MYSTERIES OF NATURE & SCIENCE

MYSTERIES OF NATURE & SCIENCE

Phillip Clarke, Elizabeth Dalby,
Laura Howell and Sarah Khan

Designed by Michael Hill, Karen Tomlins,
Ruth Russell, Laura Hammonds and Adam Constantine

Illustrations by Candice Whatmore,
Keith Furnival and Reuben Barrance

Edited by Judy Tatchell
and Kirsteen Rogers

Consultants:
Dr Tom Petersen, Revd Professor Michael J. Reiss,
Dr John Rostron, Dr Margaret Rostron,
Dr Keith Taber, Elaine Wilson

Internet links

Throughout this book, we have suggested interesting websites where you can find out more about nature and science. To visit the sites, go to the Usborne Quicklinks Website at **www.usborne-quicklinks.com** and type the keywords "nature and science". There you will find links to click on to take you to all the sites. Here are some of the things you can do on the websites:

- Make your own fish and see if it would survive in a coral reef

- Search for nocturnal animals in the Borneo rainforest

- See the steps to bird courtship dances and then try them out for yourself

- Create a clone of Mimi the mouse in a virtual laboratory

- See brain-bending, animated optical illusions – and discover how they work

- Play a game that demonstrates the mysterious effects of light-speed travel

Look for descriptions of recommended websites on the pages of this book, then go to the Usborne Quicklinks Website for links to all the sites.

INTERNET LINK

For a link to a website where you can make your own plastics in an interactive lab, go to www.usborne-quicklinks.com

Computer not essential

If you don't have access to the internet, don't worry. This book is a complete, self-contained book on its own.

www.usborne-quicklinks.com

Go to Usborne Quicklinks and enter the keywords "nature and science" for direct links to all the websites in this book.

What you need

Some websites need additional free programs, called plug-ins, to play sounds, or to show videos, animations or 3-D images. A message will appear on your screen if a site needs a particular plug-in. There is usually a button on the site that you can click on to download it. Alternatively, go to **www.usborne-quicklinks.com** and click on "Net Help". There you can find links to download plug-ins.

Internet safety

When using the internet, please follow these guidelines:

• Ask your parent's or guardian's permission before you connect to the internet.

• If you write a message in a website guest book or on a website message board, do not include any personal information such as your full name, address or telephone number, and ask an adult before you give your email address.

• If a website asks you to log in or register by typing your name or email address, ask permission of an adult first.

• If you receive an email from someone you don't know, tell an adult and do not reply to the email.

• Never arrange to meet anyone you have talked to on the internet.

Site availability

The links in Usborne Quicklinks are regularly reviewed and updated, but occasionally you may get a message that a site is unavailable. This might be temporary, so try again later, or even the next day. If any of the sites close down, we will, if possible, replace them with suitable alternatives, so you will always find an up-to-date list of sites in Usborne Quicklinks.

Notes for parents

The websites described in this book are regularly reviewed and the links in Usborne Quicklinks are updated. However, the content of a website may change at any time and Usborne Publishing is not responsible for the content on any website other than its own.

We recommend that children are supervised while on the internet, that they do not use internet chat rooms, and that you use internet filtering software to block unsuitable material. Please ensure that your children read and follow the safety guidelines printed on the left. For more information, see the "Net Help" area on the Usborne Quicklinks Website.

This tiny machine is a robotic "ant", being used in an experiment to research the reactions of a real ant.

CONTENTS

Mysteries of Nature

Mysteries of Science

MYSTERIES OF
NATURE

ANIMAL-EATING PLANTS

Most plants live in soil, and get minerals and water from it. But some plants live in such poor soil that they need food from a different source as well. Though rooted to the spot, they catch live, moving animal prey.

INTERNET LINK
For a link to a website where you can watch a movie clip of a Venus fly trap snapping shut, go to
www.usborne-quicklinks.com

Snappy trap

Venus fly traps snap shut around insects, spiders or even small frogs. Hairs on their leaves sense when something touches them. They only close around things that struggle, so don't react to things such as raindrops.

A frog lands on the leaf of a Venus fly trap, attracted by its red leaves.

If the frog touches two hairs, the trap closes loosely around it.

As the frog struggles, it stimulates the hairs again, and the trap closes tight shut.

Insects are attracted to the leaves and sweet smell of a Venus fly trap plant.

10

Slippery slope

Pitcher plants lure insects to their death by producing strong-smelling nectar. Insects go into the pitcher looking for the nectar, and fall into a mixture of water and digestive juices at the bottom. The insect's body is broken down and dissolved in this liquid, so the plant can absorb the nutrients from it.

Hood

An insect is attracted to a pitcher by the nectar produced by a gland near its hood.

Downward-pointing hairs line the pitcher's tube. The insect easily slips and tumbles in.

The pitcher hangs on a tendril that grows on the end of a leaf.

Stuck fast

Insects that are attracted to the shiny, red-tipped tentacles that cover a sundew's leaf get a nasty surprise. Instead of finding a meal of nectar, the insect becomes a meal for the sundew.

An insect lands on the sundew's leaf, and gets stuck to the sticky, sweet-smelling tentacles.

The tentacles release fluids that begin to digest the insect. The leaf slowly curls around the insect.

When the leaf opens again, the insect is completely digested. Only its hard outer case is left behind.

Bladder traps

Bladderworts float near the surface of water. Their roots are tipped by hundreds of tiny traps, called bladders.

A small creature, such as a water flea, swims past a bladder and touches sensitive hairs.

The bladder expands, and its door opens. Water rushes in, and the creature is sucked in too.

The door shuts, trapping the creature inside the bladder, where it will be digested.

11

OCEAN FEEDING

Some ocean creatures, such as great white sharks, use sheer force to catch their prey. Others use cunning, encouraging small creatures to swim straight into the jaws of death.

A great white shark strikes with such speed and force that its first bite usually kills its prey.

Unfussy eater

The great white shark is one of the most terrifying creatures in the sea. It has fearsome teeth and a powerful body. It feeds on dolphins, porpoises and fish, even other sharks. Most of all it likes to eat seals and sea lions.

The shark uses its first two rows of teeth. The back rows move up when these wear out and more will grow behind. Some sharks go through 50,000 teeth in their lifetime.

A great white shark's teeth have jagged edges to saw through flesh. A shark may have up to 3,000 teeth in its mouth at any one time.

Bubble net fishing

Humpback whales work as a team to catch fish. They round up a school of fish using streams of bubbles as nets. Then each whale expands its throat and belly, and sucks in vast amounts of water containing lots of fish.

The fish become confused by the "net" of bubbles, and seem unable to swim away.

The whales swim up through the school of fish, mouths wide open, gulping down hundreds of fish. Then they filter the water out of their mouths, leaving only the fish inside.

A group of whales sinks below a school of herrings. Each whale releases streams of bubbles.

INTERNET LINK
For a link to a website where you can see why the jaws of a shark are so deadly, go to
www.usborne-quicklinks.com

Starfish stealth

Shellfish with hinged shells are called bivalves. Their shells protect them from many enemies, but not from the harmless-looking starfish. These have powerful suckers on their arms, and an excellent sense of smell. When they sniff out a bivalve, they use their suckers to pull its shell open and get at its soft body.

A starfish grips a shellfish with its suckered arms and forces the shell open. It digests the shellfish inside by slipping its own stomach right into the shell.

Suction surprise

Frogfish crawl around coral reefs on their fins. Their rough skin helps them blend into the background. Sometimes the only visible part of a frogfish is its rod-like lure, which grows from a spine on its back and dangles in front of its mouth. The lure tricks other fish into coming closer.

The frogfish hides among coral and wiggles its lure. The lure may look like a small fish, or have a light on it, like this one.

Another fish swims closer to take a look. As it comes near, the frogfish suddenly opens its mouth to 12 times its normal size.

As water rushes into the frogfish's mouth, the other fish is sucked inside. This all happens in only a 6,000th of a second.

13

CATCHING DINNER

Reptiles, such as snakes and crocodiles, can survive for weeks, or even months, without food. Many eat huge meals when they get the chance, though. They use all their senses, skill and cunning to catch their prey.

Aerial ambush

Eyelash vipers lurk in rainforest trees, waiting for their prey. Their green, brown or yellow markings help them hide among the leaves and flowers. They can survive for up to a year between meals, but when a frog, bird or small rodent comes near, the viper strikes. It poisons the creature, then eats it.

An eyelash viper uses its tail to grip a branch while it catches and eats its prey.

Snapped up

An alligator snapping turtle is hiding at the bottom of a muddy swamp. Its shell is almost invisible.

The turtle has a piece of pink skin in its mouth, called a lure, which looks like a worm. It wiggles this to attract fish.

Any creature that comes to investigate the turtle's lure may be snapped up. It only takes a split second.

Tongue tactics

Chameleons feed on insects, frogs and small reptiles. They use their sharp eyesight to pinpoint prey. A chameleon's secret weapon is its tongue, which can extend longer than its body. The tongue forms a suction cup at the end, which sticks to the prey. It snaps back into the chameleon's mouth like elastic.

An eyelash viper is small but it can swallow prey larger than its own head. It does this by unhinging its upper and lower jaws so they can stretch apart.

A chameleon's tongue is a hollow tube that fits around a bone inside its mouth.

When muscles in the tongue pull tight around the bone, the tongue becomes very long and thin, and shoots out.

A chameleon's toes are designed for gripping branches. It also uses its tail to hang on.

Poison flows through the middle of an eyelash viper's hollow fangs. The long fangs fold back when the snake's mouth is closed.

INTERNET LINK
For a link to a website where you can watch a snake hunting its prey, go to www.usborne-quicklinks.com

Surprise snack

A Nile crocodile will eat almost anything that comes its way, such as fishes, turtles and frogs. It can even kill large animals such as wildebeest that come to the river to drink. It lurks at the water's edge and attacks with astonishing speed. It grabs the victim in its powerful jaws and drags it into the water to drown.

With one snap of its fearsome jaws, the crocodile grips its prey.

The crocodile lifts its head and tips it back before swallowing, to avoid taking in a lot of water.

A crocodile lurks silently in the water, with only its eyes poking above the surface.

FOOD ON THE MOVE

Birds catch food using only their beaks or their feet. They must strike quickly, or go hungry. Some use speed, aerobatic skills and keen eyesight to catch prey. Others use stealth, cunning and even bait, to lure their prey within striking distance.

Fly fishing

Kingfishers are small but spectacular hunters. They catch insects in mid-air and dive into rivers to catch fish. A kingfisher dives so fast that it looks like a brilliant blue streak. Its beak is exactly the right shape to snatch a slippery fish from the water.

INTERNET LINK
For a link to a website where you can watch owls and kingfishers catching their prey, go to www.usborne-quicklinks.com

A kingfisher scans the water for fish, from a perch or while hovering. If it sees a fish, it goes into a dive.

It dives at an angle of 45°, making quick wingbeats to speed itself as it nears the surface of the water.

The kingfisher closes its eyes as it hits the water, and grabs the fish in its beak. It swallows it whole.

This brown pelican's pouch is stretched out of shape by the big fish it has caught.

Group fishing

A pelican has a large beak with a stretchy pouch to hold a big catch of fish. Instead of fishing alone, pelicans work in teams. This gives each pelican a better chance of a good meal.

The pelicans herd fish ahead of them into shallow water, by flapping their wings.

When the fish are in shallow water, the pelicans scoop them up in their huge beaks.

A pelican tips its beak down to let water run out before tipping it back to swallow.

Wait or bait

A green heron stands like a statue at the edge of the water, waiting for an unwary fish to swim by. If a fish does arrive, the heron attacks swiftly. If no fish comes along, the heron will try to attract one using bait.

A heron places its bait. This may be an insect or a small object like a feather.

Fish nearby are interested in the bait and come to take a closer look.

The heron strikes like lightning, spearing the fish on the end of its pointed beak.

Terrible talons

Owls have long claws, called talons, designed to kill. An owl tears its food apart with its beak and talons, or swallows small animals whole. Later, it spits out any body parts that it can't digest, such as bones or fur, in the form of a pellet.

Super senses

Owls hunt at night. They have super-keen hearing that can pick up the rustle of a mouse moving on the ground, from the top of a tall tree. An owl's ears are on the sides of its head, but face to the front. In the picture above, you can see two dish shapes on the owl's face which help to channel sounds into its ears.

This mouse is carrying a berry for its own meal. It hasn't heard the owl swooping down on it.

MAMMALS' MEALS

If an animal doesn't eat, it dies. Stealth and speed are the secret weapons of many hungry mammals. These are animals that have hair on their bodies and feed their babies with milk. Some use special tools, such as a long tongue or claw, to find food.

Vampire bats hunt at night.

Hidden treats

An aye-aye's special tool is its long, bony middle finger, tipped with a curved claw. It taps on a tree, listening for the hollow sounds of insects' tunnels. It then chews away the bark and probes for its prey.

Aerial anteater

Tamanduas are anteaters that live in trees. They eat ants, termites, bees and honey. They have a clever way of making sure their food supply doesn't run out.

A tamandua rips open a nest of insects with its claws. It uses its tongue to lick up the occupants.

It doesn't entirely destroy the nest, though. It lets some insects survive so they can rebuild the nest and colony.

This means that the tamandua can come back later for another feast of insects from the same nest.

An aye-aye uses its long, bony middle finger to scoop insects and grubs out of the hole it has made.

Blood lappers

Vampire bats are the only mammals that feed on other animals' blood. A bat needs to eat at least every two nights to survive and may spend two hours feeding from a single animal. It bites a hole in the animal's skin with its long, sharp front teeth. The hole fills with blood, which the bat laps up.

Vampire bats use hearing and smell to find sleeping animals to feed from.

Tall order

Giraffes are designed to reach the parts of trees that other animals – apart from elephants – can't. With their extra-long necks and legs, giraffes feed on the juicy leaves of acacia and mimosa trees. They need to feed for up to 20 hours every day.

A giraffe's tongue can be over 50cm (20in) long – even longer than an anteater's.

The giraffe can grab leaves with its rubbery upper lip. But if the tree is thorny, it uses its long tongue to pluck leaves from between the thorns.

Surprise attack

To catch food, tigers use stealth. A tiger tracks down its prey (deer, wild pigs and rodents), using its excellent vision, hearing and sense of smell. It then takes its time moving quietly into an attacking position. When it is within 25m (80ft) of its victim, it charges.

A tiger can easily leap up to 6m (20ft). To kill its prey, it bites the back of an animal's neck, or its throat.

INTERNET LINK
For a link to a website where you can find lots of interesting vampire bat facts, go to www.usborne-quicklinks.com

FEEDING FEATURES

Insects and spiders have specially designed bodies to cope with the kind of food they eat. They also have clever ways of catching their prey.

An orange orb spider lies in wait on its web in the Amazon rainforest.

Sticky situation

The silk that spiders use to spin their webs is extremely thin and very stretchy. Some of this silk is smooth, for the spider to walk on. Some is sticky, to trap passing insects. The silk is made in glands called spinnerets. It leaves the spider's body as a liquid that hardens in the air.

A spider starts its web by spinning the first thread into the air. The wind carries it to a second point, where it sticks. The spider carefully walks across this thread.

The spider walks back and forth along the thread, making it thicker. It then spins a second thread to make a "Y" shape. Gradually, it adds more threads from the central point.

The web now looks like the spokes of a bicycle wheel. The spider spirals around the spokes, spinning more silk as it goes, to complete the web.

Some orb spiders make a new web every day. Before they make a new web, they eat the old one, to avoid wasting the protein that makes up the silk.

Spider silk is five times stronger than steel wire would be – if steel wire could be made as thin.

Eating out

There are around six million different kinds of insects. They eat a huge variety of food, from flower nectar and plant juices to dead animals.

Insects' mouthparts are designed to cope with their different diets.

A moth's tube-like mouth, called a proboscis, is usually curled up. The moth uncurls it to suck flower nectar.

The long, tube-like part of a cicada's mouth drills into plants. It can then suck up the juices inside.

A housefly's mouthparts have a sponge-like end. This mops up food softened by the fly's saliva.

Beetles have mouthparts that can bite and chew. They feed mainly on dead plants or animals.

Fungus farmers

Leaf-cutter ants grow their own food. They strip leaves from nearby trees, cut the leaves into pieces and carry them back to their underground nest. There, other ants bite the pieces of leaf into smaller pieces and mix them with saliva. A kind of fungus grows on this leaf mixture, and it's this fungus that the ants eat.

This small ant's job is to defend the larger ant from a type of fly that attacks ants while they are carrying leaves and unable to defend themselves.

A colony of leaf-cutter ants can strip a tree of leaves in a single day.

This ant is carrying a piece of leaf back to the nest. The leaf may be two or three times as heavy as the ant.

INTERNET LINK
For a link to a website where you can see close-ups of bugs and find out how they feed, go to www.usborne-quicklinks.com

21

PLANTS ON THE MOVE

It might be hard to believe that plants move – but most can move parts of themselves, a little. Many grow or move in the direction of things they need, such as sunlight or water.

Dandelion seeds are designed to move on the wind, so that they can be carried to new homes.

Sun lover

For a plant to bend, turn its head or grow in a different direction, the cells in the affected part have to change shape. Plant movements like this are called tropisms. Some tropisms, such as the one below, might happen in minutes.

As the Sun rises, the stem of a sunflower bends so the flower head faces the Sun.

Cells in the side of the stem facing away from the Sun expand to make this happen.

The sunflowers follow the Sun's movement across the sky. This is called heliotropism.

This vine grows tendrils from its stem or leaves. When it touches something, the tendril curls around it for support.

This is a passionflower vine. It can grow to over 9m (30ft) long.

Cunning creeper

Vines have roots in the ground but cling to other plants for support. They grow as fast as they can in the direction of the most sunlight. Because they don't support themselves, they can put all their energy into growing longer.

Secret of the beans

A "jumping bean" appears to move and jiggle on its own. It is really the seed capsule of a kind of Mexican shrub – with a caterpillar inside. When the caterpillar moves, so does the bean.

A jumping bean moth lays its eggs on the seed pod of a Mexican jumping bean plant.

When the eggs hatch, the jumping bean caterpillars eat their way into the pod, to feed on the seed capsules inside.

The seed pods turn brown and fall to the ground. They break open and the seed capsules scatter. A capsule with a caterpillar inside is called a jumping bean.

A cloud of spores is freed when the fungus is touched, for example by a raindrop.

INTERNET LINK
For a link to a website where you can find more information about Mexican jumping beans, go to
www.usborne-quicklinks.com

Wind travel

A ripe puffball fungus is filled with tiny seeds called spores. These are carried away from the fungus by the wind. If the conditions are right, new fungi grow where the spores land. In this way, each generation of fungi moves to a different place.

MOVING THROUGH WATER

Not everything that lives in the ocean swims like a fish. There are lots of other ways of moving through the water, including hitching a ride.

Sucker fish

A remora is a fish with a sucker near the top of its head. It can attach this sucker to a shark, ray, turtle or even a boat. It is pulled through the water and feeds on scraps of food dropped by its host. It finds more food this way than it would on its own.

This remora has stuck itself to the underside of a turtle. The faster the turtle swims, the tighter the remora grips.

A remora has a ridged sucker. When the ridges are raised against a surface, they grip very strongly.

Helpful passenger

Sea anemones usually attach themselves to rock or coral. They catch food in their tentacles. One way to get a ride to a different place where there might be more food, is to hitch a lift with a hermit crab.

This hermit crab has three sea anemones attached to it. They feed on scraps of food dropped by the crab.

Sea anemones
Crab's body and legs
Crab's eyes
Crab's shell

Sea anemones protect the crab. They are poisonous and also help to hide it.

Super swimmer

A squid can move very fast in any direction, using jet propulsion. Its fins act as stabilizers. It also uses its fins to swim more slowly. A squid can swim for long periods of time over great distances in its search for food. It starts off with jet propulsion, then switches to fin-power.

A squid's body is supported inside by a stiff rod called a pen, made of a substance called chitin.

Water in
Funnel
Water in

Water out

The squid takes water into its strong, muscular body. It angles its funnel, ready to move.

It squeezes water out through its funnel. This jet-propels it in the opposite direction.

INTERNET LINKS
For links to websites where you can watch sea creatures on the move and see a giant squid, go to
www.usborne-quicklinks.com

Speed or steer?

Fish are specially designed to cope with moving through water, which is denser than air. Some are built for speed, but can't rapidly change direction. Others don't move fast, but are able to twist and turn between rocks, reefs and plants.

Eels use their back and underside fins to move. They are able to back their long bodies into narrow caves.

Parrotfish use their side fins to paddle. They can twist and turn easily, weaving between coral reefs.

Sharks use their tail fins to propel themselves. They can move very fast but are unable to turn quickly or swim in reverse.

25

GLIDING AND SLIDING

Reptiles and amphibians, such as snakes, lizards and frogs, move in a variety of ways. Some can even travel across the surface of water or soft, shifting sands. Others, like the tree frog on the right, can glide through the air.

This tree frog is 1/3 actual size.

Moving around can take a long time for a small animal in a rainforest. A Wallace's tree frog saves time by gliding up to 15m (50ft) between trees.

Sideways motion

Sidewinders get their name from the way they move. They live in sandy deserts where the surface is scorching hot and slippery. The sidewinder moves by looping its body sideways, which helps it get a grip on the surface of the sand. It also means that less of its body touches the hot sand at any time.

The frog's toes are very long, and webbing between them acts like a sail or parachute. Pads on its toes grip firmly when it lands.

As it throws its body sideways, a sidewinder leaves distinctive tracks in the desert sand.

Tail talents

Crested geckos jump between trees to get around in the rainforest. A gecko uses its grasping tail like a fifth limb to cling onto branches, or like a rudder to help it balance and steer in the air.

INTERNET LINK
For a link to a website where you can find out more about the secret of a gecko's sticky feet, go to www.usborne-quicklinks.com

The underside of each foot is covered in two million hairs.

Sticky feet

Geckos are able to walk on vertical surfaces and even upside-down, as if their feet were covered in glue. In fact, each foot is covered in millions of tiny hairs, which bond with surfaces to help the gecko cling on.

There are tiny forces of electrical attraction between the hairs on a gecko's foot and the surfaces it walks on. This makes them stick together.

No time to sink

Basilisk lizards can walk on water. This is possible because they are light, with large, fringed feet. They move too fast to sink. If a lizard can't escape on the surface of the water, it may let itself sink and try swimming to safety instead.

Basilisk lizards can run at speeds of up to 12kph (7.5mph) – about twice as fast as a person walking quickly.

AIR, LAND AND WATER

All birds have wings but not all birds are able, or choose, to fly. Some prefer to walk or swim, for instance. Birds that do fly have different ways of taking off and staying up in the air.

Lift-off

The bigger the bird, the bigger the wingspan it needs to achieve lift-off.

Swans are among the largest waterbirds. As well as big wings, they need a running start of up to 40m (130ft), before they can take off. They run into the wind, to speed up the flow of air over their wings. This helps lift them into the air.

A swan runs across the surface of the water on its large, webbed feet, getting up speed for take-off.

INTERNET LINK
For a link to a website where you can go on a virtual flight with a golden eagle, go to www.usborne-quicklinks.com

Aerial agility

Tiny hummingbirds depend on their agility in the air to outwit large predators such as hawks. Their wings beat up to 90 times each second. A hummingbird can fly in any direction and can even hover in mid-air. They rarely walk along the ground, but they do perch briefly on branches or on the ground in between flights.

Hummingbirds need a lot of energy to maintain their high-speed life. They feed almost constantly on sugary flower nectar.

Water walker

African jacanas are quite heavy birds but they are able to run across the surface of water, supported only by delicate plants such as water lilies. They can do this because they have incredibly long toes, which spread their weight across a large area. They don't often walk on land – their long toes make this difficult. But they can fly, and they are excellent swimmers and divers.

Water plants help support a jacana as it skips across the surface.

Compared to its body size, the African jacana has the largest toes of any bird.

Speed swimming

Chinstrap penguins waddle awkwardly on their feet over the ice. On snow they find it easier, and quicker, to "toboggan" on their chests, pushing themselves along with their wings. They are most agile in the water. They can swim fast enough to outpace leopard seals, and can leap out of the water onto ice floes up to 2m (6.5ft) high.

Chinstrap penguins use their feet as powerful paddles in the water. Their wings act as flippers when they are swimming, to help them steer.

MADE TO MOVE

Mammals have developed some amazing ways of getting from one place to another, both on the ground and in the air.

Jumping power

Kangaroos are shy and usually stay hidden during the day. But at night, they leap across the Australian landscape, looking for fresh grass to eat. They can reach speeds of up to 48kph (30mph) – and amazingly, the faster they go, the less energy they use up.

This is possible because when it is jumping, a kangaroo's legs act like springs. The energy from the first jump stays in the kangaroo's legs and is used to power the next jump. This jump then helps to power the next, and so on.

A kangaroo stretches its tail out behind when it jumps, to help it balance.

Kangaroos can jump up to 3m (10ft) high.

Kangaroos' legs are very well-suited to jumping but this means that they can't walk very well.

INTERNET LINKS
For links to websites where you can watch slide shows and videos about mammals and see how they move, go to **www.usborne-quicklinks.com**

Hidden wings

A sugar glider conceals a secret method of movement. Two flaps of skin between its front and back legs can be stretched to form "wings" called gliding membranes. The sugar glider uses the membranes to parachute from one tree to another, in its search for insects, nectar and sap to eat.

When a sugar glider is resting, the skin flaps are barely visible.

When it is in the air, the skin flaps stretch. Muscles in them let the glider steer.

Born to run

A cheetah has a long stride, made possible by its very flexible spine. As it reaches out with its front legs, the spine curves down.

As the front legs push back, the spine curves up. This lets the back legs come all the way forward, ready to push off again.

Cheetahs are the fastest animals on land, with a top speed of 115kph (70mph). Every part of a cheetah's streamlined body is designed for speed. It has large paw pads and claws to grip the ground firmly. Its skeleton is strong and very light. Its extra-large nostrils and lungs can take in lots of oxygen when the cheetah is running.

Kangaroos have sharp claws on their small front paws, for fighting.

Red kangaroos are the largest marsupials – these are mammals with pouches for their young.

A kangaroo can travel up to 9m (30ft) in one bound.

31

WINGS AND LEGS

Some insects are capable of truly amazing feats of flight, from displays of speed and agility to incredible endurance. Other small creatures can make great leaps to catch prey – or to avoid being caught themselves.

Monarch migration

Every winter, millions of monarch butterflies leave their homes in North America and travel south to Mexico where the weather is warmer. The following summer, they return north to breed.

This kind of return trip, to find warmer weather, is called a migration. Many other butterflies spend the winter as eggs or larvae. They emerge as adults in spring.

Monarch butterflies stop to drink nectar to fuel their journey. To save energy, they try to glide as much as possible.

The red lines show some of the monarchs' routes from North America to Mexico – up to 4,800km (3,000 miles).

Jumping spiders have good eyesight so they hit their target.

Long leap

Jumping spiders can jump 50 times the length of their own bodies to catch prey. They don't have very big leg muscles, though. Instead, a spider jumps by lifting up its front legs and then contracting the muscles in its body. This raises its blood pressure, which forces fluid into the back legs. They straighten very quickly, propelling the spider into the air.

Fantastic fliers

Dragonflies are among the fastest flying insects. They can reach speeds of up to 95kph (60mph). They can also hover – useful while they seek out prey with their sharp eyes – and can dart in different directions. They do all this in spite of having a primitive wing design that has not changed for millions of years.

A dragonfly's body is tilted so that its legs hang below its jaws. Here, it is about to catch a mosquito in its basket of legs.

It eats the mosquito as it flies, with its strong, biting mouthparts.

Dragonflies have two pairs of wings. The front pair can move independently of the back pair.

INTERNET LINK
For a link to a website where you can find out about monarch butterflies, go to www.usborne-quicklinks.com

Muscle power

Grasshoppers have several ways of moving. Like most insects, they have six legs and two pairs of wings, and can crawl or fly. They also have very long, muscular back legs, which let them make incredible jumps. If a grasshopper were the size of a person, it would be able to jump 40m (130ft) from a standstill.

Preparing to jump, the grasshopper crouches, with its back legs folded.

The leg muscles contract and the legs straighten, launching the grasshopper.

PLANTS FIGHT BACK

Plants can't run away from their enemies but many defend themselves fiercely. Some even produce poisons that can kill animals that try to eat them.

Thorny issue

Umbrella thorn acacias are the most common trees on the African grasslands. Grazing animals would devour their juicy leaves, if they weren't protected by thorns. The acacias have two different kinds of thorns – long, straight, white thorns and small, brown, hooked thorns. Each kind of thorn puts off different animals.

An acacia's thorns are arranged in clusters.

The only animal with a mouth tough enough to deal with the acacia's thorns is a giraffe.

Fearsome fungi

Some mushrooms are armed with deadly poisons. The most poisonous mushroom in the world is the death cap. People sometimes mistake this for an edible mushroom, with fatal results. A relative of the death cap is the poisonous fly agaric, shown in the photograph. Every part of this mushroom is poisonous, even its spores. Its bright cap is easy to recognize, though.

The white scales on this fly agaric's cap and the frill on its stalk are leftovers from the covering it had when it was growing.

Death caps can be difficult to identify. They may look like some types of edible mushrooms.

Prickly protection

Cactus spines put off most grazing animals. Prickly pear cacti, like the one in this photo, have two kinds of spines – large, widely-spaced spikes, and clumps of tiny spines which irritate if they get under skin. Some animals, such as iguanas, have mouths tough enough to eat the cacti anyway. Rabbits, also, are able to nibble the juicy flesh between the spines.

Many cacti grow in deserts. Desert animals eat them because they are moist and full of nutrients.

Some birds build their nests inside the stems of cacti. The spines give them protection from predators.

Bolshy bush

Creosote bushes are very successful desert plants. Their waxy leaves help to stop them from losing too much water. The leaves also taste terrible to grazing animals. The bushes compete against other desert plants by giving off poisons from their roots. This prevents other plants from growing too near and taking valuable water.

The oldest-known creosote bush is 9,400 years old.

New shoots grow up around the outside of a creosote bush. Eventually the middle part dies, leaving a ring of new growth, which is all part of the original plant.

The prickly pear's large spines keep most animals at a distance.

The small spines, called glochids, break off easily if they are touched.

INTERNET LINK
For a link to a website where you can explore a fungus museum, go to www.usborne-quicklinks.com

WATER WEAPONS

Some ocean creatures are able to attack and kill much faster, stronger animals, or defend themselves against animals several times their own size. Many use deadly stings or even electric shocks.

Terrible tentacles

Jellyfish have tentacles which they use to catch small fish or other creatures to eat. The tentacles are covered in stinging cells. These deliver powerful poison to the victims which are usually killed or paralyzed immediately. The jellyfish has "arms" which move food caught by its tentacles to its mouth, in the middle of its body.

A stinging cell consists of a sensitive hair, a lid, and a nematocyst, which fires like a miniature harpoon if the hair is touched.

This is a sea nettle jellyfish. When its tentacles sting, they also stick tight to the victim, trapping it completely.

INTERNET LINK
For a link to a website where you can see how different kinds of jellyfish move, go to www.usborne-quicklinks.com

Small but deadly

A blue-ringed octopus is only the size of a golfball but it is one of the most poisonous creatures in the sea. It contains enough poison to kill 25 men, and there is no known antidote. Because it is so small, it can be difficult to spot before it's too late.

A blue-ringed octopus usually blends into the sand and rocks on the bottom of the sea.

If it is agitated, for example if it is about to attack, it turns bright yellow with blue ring markings.

Final attack

Porcupine fish defend themselves against enemies by taking water into their stomachs and inflating to twice their normal size. They can even inflate in a predator's throat, if they have already been swallowed. This doesn't save the porcupine fish, but it does kill its predator as well.

A porcupine fish's spines usually lie flat. As it inflates, they stick out and this scares many attackers off. An inflated fish can't swim fast, so it just hopes its attacker will give up.

Shock tactics

Torpedo rays use electric shocks to stun fish and shellfish. They have two electrical organs near their heads that work like batteries. These can give electric shocks powerful enough to kill a fish – but not a person.

A torpedo ray has electrical organs near its head. They make up about one-sixth of its total body weight.

POISONING AND SQUEEZING

Many snakes use poison, called venom, to attack or to defend themselves. They bite their enemies. Other snakes squeeze their victims to death. Some rainforest frogs have poisonous skins to protect themselves.

This is a strawberry poison dart frog. Its bright markings warn predators to stay away, because its skin is covered with a poisonous slime.

This frog lives in the South American rainforest.

Poisoned skin

Poison dart frogs have moist skin that is covered in a poisonous slime. Some rainforest people coat the tips of blow-gun darts with this poison and use them for hunting small animals. One frog may produce enough poison to coat the tips of 50 darts.

Spitting snake

If it is threatened, a spitting cobra can shoot a spray of poison, or venom, at the eyes of an enemy. It can hit its target up to 2m (7ft) away. The venom causes temporary blindness, so the snake can dart in and deliver a poisonous bite. It's the bite that actually kills the enemy.

Muscles contract and pump venom from a sac through holes in the cobra's fangs.

The snake breathes air out. This passes through the venom, making a spray.

The spray blinds the victim. The cobra then attacks with its teeth, injecting more venom.

Brutal bite

Gila monsters are one of two kinds of poisonous lizards. They live in the desert and catch rodents and birds. They inject venom by chewing on their victims' flesh.

Venom from glands in the gila monster's mouth trickles along the grooves in its teeth.

INTERNET LINK
For a link to a website with a life-size interactive tour of a king cobra, go to www.usborne-quicklinks.com

Tight squeeze

Some snakes, like pythons and boas, are not poisonous. Instead, they use muscle power to crush their victims to death. When the victim has suffocated, the snake eats it.

This python is squeezing to death a victim larger than itself.

Fearsome fangs

The fangs of poisonous snakes come in many shapes and sizes. Some are grooved, others are hollow. Non-poisonous snakes don't have fangs. Their teeth are short, for holding onto prey.

Cobras have short, hollow fangs which are fixed at the front of their mouths. The fangs inject venom.

Vipers have long, hollow, front fangs. These fold flat against the roof of the snake's mouth when they are not being used.

Boomslangs have grooved fangs at the back of their mouths. Venom drips along the grooves as the snake chews its victim.

Pythons are non-poisonous. Their teeth are short and curved, for gripping their prey.

39

BIRD BATTLES

Most birds defend the areas where they breed or feed. These areas are called territories. Disputes over territories can end in dramatic and vicious fighting – or even death.

Although snowy egrets have long, sharp beaks and fight often, they don't usually injure each other.

Beak wrestling

Male snowy egrets defend quite large territories. A bird performs displays in its own territory to keep other males away and also to attract females. When two male egrets fight, they wrestle with their beaks. This helps them decide which bird is the stronger, without either getting badly injured.

Territorial tapping

Male woodpeckers use sound to communicate with rival males and to attract females. Instead of singing, they tap out messages with their beaks on the bark of trees. Woodpeckers learn to recognize the different rhythms made by other birds, telling them to stay away or inviting them closer.

To make a loud tap, a woodpecker hits the tree hard with its beak.

The woodpecker also uses its beak to scoop insects out of tree bark.

It lives in a nest, carved with its beak out of a tree trunk.

Fighting for fish

Going into battle against a bald eagle, with its fearsome beak and talons, is a risky thing to do – even for another bald eagle. But sometimes they do fight among themselves, to claim territory or just to steal a rival's fish. Fights over territory sometimes end in death for the losing eagle.

Bald eagles sometimes use their sharp beaks and talons against each other, to steal food.

INTERNET LINK
For a link to a website with more about bald eagles, go to www.usborne-quicklinks.com

Safety in numbers

Gannets nest in huge colonies of thousands of birds but they only do so because it gives greater protection from enemies. They are not really sociable or cooperative. They share their feeding territory but each bird fiercely defends its own tiny breeding territory. It will attack other bird or animal intruders.

Warning song

Male European robins are fierce defenders of their territory. They will viciously attack any intruders, especially at nesting time. Robins sing songs to warn off other males. This means they don't need to patrol their territory all the time.

A robin's red breast gives him away if he dares to enter a rival male's territory.

A gannet defends its tiny breeding territory against another gannet. It attacks the intruder with its sharp beak to scare it away.

TAKE ME ON

Many mammals fight among themselves, trying to impress a mate. Some of their contests turn into spectacular displays of physical strength and superiority – sometimes ending in death.

The fighting life

Wolves live in groups called packs. Both males and females fight to decide who is top wolf of the pack. The top male and female mate with each other. Wolves from different packs fight when they meet, and some wolves may be killed.

These wolves from the same pack are play-fighting. They do this from an early age, preparing for real fights.

> **INTERNET LINK**
> For a link to a website where you can read a photo-journal about wolves and listen to them howl, go to
> www.usborne-quicklinks.com

Poisonous platypus

The duck-billed platypus is one of only three poisonous mammals. The males have horn-like spurs on their back legs. These spurs are hollow and are connected to a poison gland. The poison is strong enough to kill small animals. Scientists think that platypuses use their spurs to fight with rival males over females or territory.

A platypus has webbed feet for swimming. Only the back legs have spurs.

Brand new headgear

Every year, a bull moose grows a new set of antlers. This takes a lot of energy and the moose needs extra minerals. It gets these by eating willow shoots, bones and even old antlers. Usually the moose with the biggest antlers gets the most females – the males rarely fight with their antlers. This avoids unnecessary injury.

At the start of the summer, a bull moose's antlers are just small, velvety knobs. They grow quickly – about 1cm (0.5in), or 0.5kg (1lb), every day.

The velvety skin on the growing antlers supplies them with blood and minerals. When the antlers are fully grown, the moose rubs the velvet off against trees and rocks.

Antlers are made of bone. A bull moose's antlers may span 1.8m (6ft) and weigh as much as 36kg (80lbs). At the end of the summer, the antlers drop off.

Triumphant tusks

Walrus tusks have several uses. They are good for making holes in the Arctic ice, and they help a walrus to pull itself out of the sea when it returns to land. They also help male walruses to decide which is the most dominant – the bigger the tusks, the more important the walrus.

Only walruses with similar-sized tusks fight, to decide which is superior.

A walrus's tusks are enlarged front teeth. They may be up to 90cm (3ft) long.

INSECT ATTACK

Insects are able to attack enemies much larger than themselves. Many use chemical warfare, such as poisons and burning liquids, to defend themselves or catch prey.

Lurking lion

The larvae of some kinds of lacewings are called ant-lions, because they prey ferociously on ants. Ant-lions live in sandy areas. They dig cone-shaped traps to catch their prey.

An ant-lion buries itself almost completely in a pit in the sand. Only its pincer-like jaws stick out.

It flicks sand at passing ants to make them lose their footing and slide down the sloping sides of the pit.

The ant-lion strikes with a snap of its jaws. It devours the ant, then rebuilds its trap to wait for more prey.

Beetle bang

A bombardier beetle can aim a boiling-hot spray of toxic liquid to fend off an attacker. The spray shoots out with a loud bang. The chemicals in the spray are mixed together just before the beetle fires it. They react with each other to make the explosive noise and generate heat.

A beetle uses its antennae to sense its surroundings by touch and smell.

This beetle is spraying an attacking frog. This will give it time to unfurl its wings and fly to safety.

The spray leaves the beetle's body as hot as boiling water. Amazingly, it doesn't seem to burn the beetle.

Smelly spray

Darkling beetles use a spray of terrible-smelling liquid to defend themselves. If they are threatened, they crouch down, raise their back ends into the air and prepare to release their spray. Many animals avoid them because of their smell, but they are preyed on by owls, toads and skunks.

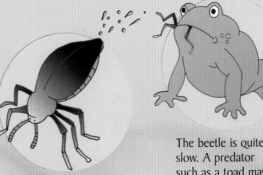

A darkling beetle tips its back end up and sprays an attacker with a foul-smelling liquid.

The beetle is quite slow. A predator such as a toad may be able to swallow it before it has time to spray.

A grasshopper mouse has a clever way of disarming the beetle. It pushes its dangerous back end into the ground and nibbles the front end.

INTERNET LINK
For a link to a website where you can find out more about the amazing bombardier beetle, go to www.usborne-quicklinks.com

An assassin bug holds its prey with its front legs and pierces it with its sharp beak.

Assassin bugs have bright markings which warn other insects to beware of their poison.

Insect hitman

Assassin bugs get their name because of the way they ambush other small creatures. An assassin bug strikes quickly, grabbing its prey with its two front legs and using its sharp beak to inject saliva. The saliva immobilizes the victim and begins to dissolve its tissues. The bug can then suck up its victim's remains through its beak.

This assassin bug is eating a crab spider. Sometimes assassin bugs even eat each other.

TRICKY PLANTS

Some plants use tricks and disguises to attract helpful small creatures, while others try to hide away for fear of being eaten. A few plants fight back against grazing animals with painful, acidic stings.

Living stones

Living stones come out of hiding when they flower – the bright flowers attract insects.

In the desert, juicy plants can be a source of moisture for thirsty animals. But living stone plants look just like small pebbles, blending in with their dry, rocky surroundings. Only a small part of the plant sticks up above the surface of the ground.

The only two parts of the living stone that poke above ground are the fleshy leaves.

The egg trick

Butterflies try to lay their eggs where their caterpillars will have plenty of food when they hatch. A good place is on the leaf of a tasty plant. To avoid becoming caterpillar food, some plants fight back.

Heliconius butterflies lay their eggs on passionflower vines, on the underside of the leaves.

When the eggs hatch, the caterpillars devour the plant, killing it in the process.

Butterflies tend not to lay eggs on leaves where there are eggs already. So one type of vine grows false eggs on its leaves, tricking butterflies into leaving it alone.

Orchid or wasp?

Many orchids look like bees or wasps in order to attract them to help spread their pollen. A hammer orchid looks as if it has a female wasp perching on it, and releases a smell like a female wasp. Male wasps are attracted to the orchid, and even try to mate with it.

A male wasp comes in to land on a hammer orchid flower. As it does so, it will pick up pollen.

Painful lesson

Making stings uses up a lot of a plant's energy, which might otherwise be put into growing. But this is what protects stinging nettles from being eaten by grazing animals. Once they have been stung, animals learn to recognize stinging nettles and avoid them.

Dead nettles have no stings, but their leaves are a similar shape to the leaves of stinging nettles. Animals learn to avoid both.

INTERNET LINK

For a link to a website where you can find out how plants stop animals from feeding on them, go to www.usborne-quicklinks.com

This magnification of part of a stinging nettle shows its needle-like hairs. If anything touches them, they snap off, releasing a stinging acid.

SURVIVAL TRICKS

Many underwater creatures use camouflage to hide themselves from predators or prey. Others have early warning systems that give them time to escape or to unleash weapons on their attackers.

The pink part shows the scorpion fish in the photo. The yellow part is the coral.

Lying in wait

A scorpionfish lurks on a coral reef near the shallow sea bottom. Its warty, lumpy, speckled skin is the ultimate camouflage. It stays quite still, waiting to prey on smaller fish and crabs which wander past. It fears no predators – as well as being perfectly camouflaged, it is also extremely poisonous.

Scallop sight

Unlike other shellfish, scallops have eyes around the edges of their shells. These eyes are not powerful enough to make out any details but they enable the scallop to sense changes in light, or movements in the water nearby. If a predator approaches, the scallop may have time to swim away.

Scorpion fish are able to change their mottled markings to blend with their surroundings.

A scallop has between 50 and 100 eyes. If they sense movement, the scallop closes its shell.

If a shadow is cast over the scallop, it propels itself away through the water by flapping the two halves of its shell.

Dragon of the sea

Sea dragons shimmy through the water, trailing leafy flaps from their bodies and looking just like seaweed. Their camouflage lets them swim unnoticed, sucking up tiny creatures into their toothless mouths as they go. They are slow but have few predators, as their soft bodies are protected by bony plates.

Sea dragons swim by flapping tiny, translucent fins along their bodies.

INTERNET LINK
For a link to a website where you can choose which sea creature has the best camouflage, go to
www.usborne-quicklinks.com

One-sided fish

Flatfish swim on one side on the sea bottom. Both eyes are on the side that faces up. But young flatfish hatch with an eye on each side. It takes a few weeks for one eye to move around as the fishes change into their adult form.

Young flatfish look like other fishes, with an eye on each side of the head.

By six weeks old, both eyes are on the same side.

Cucumber surprise

Sea cucumbers can't move quickly but they can defend themselves in an unusual way. They spit out their internal organs, which confuses and even temporarily blinds a predator. Amazingly, the sea cucumber survives and the lost organs regrow in a few weeks.

A disturbed sea cucumber shoots out sticky, poisonous streams of internal organs at a crab.

49

FIGHTING BACK

Reptiles have tough skins for protection, and unusual fighting weapons. Horned lizards can even squirt their own blood to put an enemy off. Reptiles and amphibians are also masters of camouflage.

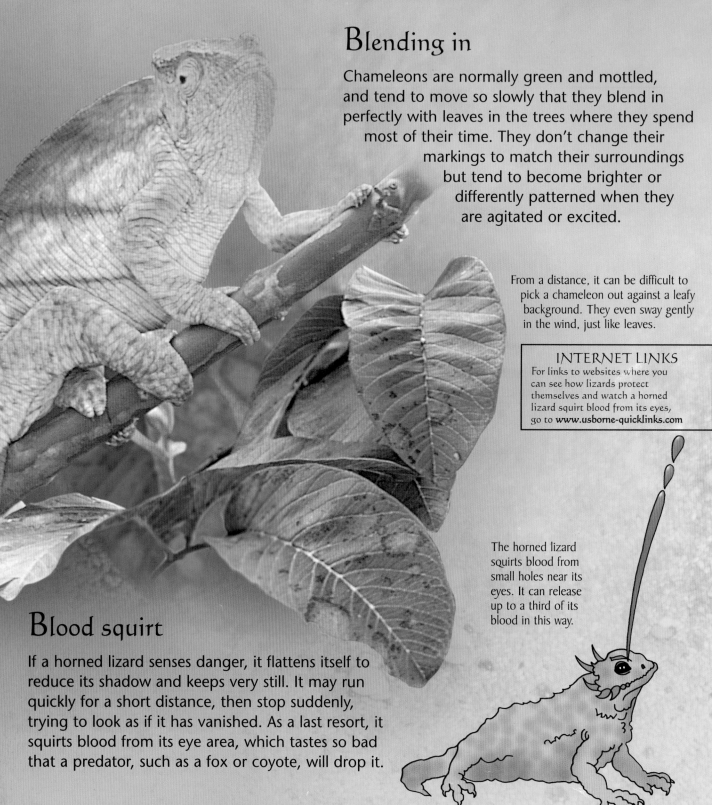

Blending in

Chameleons are normally green and mottled, and tend to move so slowly that they blend in perfectly with leaves in the trees where they spend most of their time. They don't change their markings to match their surroundings but tend to become brighter or differently patterned when they are agitated or excited.

From a distance, it can be difficult to pick a chameleon out against a leafy background. They even sway gently in the wind, just like leaves.

INTERNET LINKS
For links to websites where you can see how lizards protect themselves and watch a horned lizard squirt blood from its eyes, go to www.usborne-quicklinks.com

The horned lizard squirts blood from small holes near its eyes. It can release up to a third of its blood in this way.

Blood squirt

If a horned lizard senses danger, it flattens itself to reduce its shadow and keeps very still. It may run quickly for a short distance, then stop suddenly, trying to look as if it has vanished. As a last resort, it squirts blood from its eye area, which tastes so bad that a predator, such as a fox or coyote, will drop it.

Defensive tactics

Australian thorny devils may not look very tasty, with their all-over spiny covering, but they are still in danger from large birds. Apart from its prickles, a thorny devil has a few other tricks.

When scared or cold (and so unable to run fast), the thorny devil's markings become duller and help to camouflage it.

The thorny devil can inflate itself by taking gulps of air. This may deter a predator from trying to swallow it.

It can stick up a spiny bump on its back, to look like a false head, and confuse predators.

Hard to swallow

Armadillo lizards can't run very fast so they have to use other methods to outwit predators such as snakes or birds. They can, with a little effort, make themselves completely unswallowable.

A lizard may try to fight off attackers by rolling its tail up to form a club, which it can hit with.

It may curl up into a ball, with its spiny, bony back facing out. Its soft tummy is protected on the inside.

The lizard may squeeze into a rocky crevice to escape. It raises its spines so that it can't be pulled out from its hiding place.

Double camouflage

A bullfrog's green skin helps camouflage it in its swampy home, especially when it is submerged in duckweed with only its eyes showing above the water. From here, the frog is in the perfect position to stalk insect prey such as fireflies, bees and crickets. At the same time, it is hidden from its own predators such as herons, owls and hawks.

This bullfrog is well-hidden from birds, but there is also danger from muskrats, fishes and even larger bullfrogs under the water.

STAYING SAFE

Some birds put a lot of effort into building nests in places that are hard to reach. Others just make a small scrape in the ground to lay their eggs. Both adults and babies use camouflage and other tactics to protect themselves from attack.

Hidden in the sand

Black skimmers live near water and make very shallow nests on sandy beaches for their eggs. Their chicks are vulnerable out in the open, so they rely on excellent camouflage to protect themselves.

INTERNET LINKS
For links to websites with video clips of gull chicks feeding and a ptarmigan digging in the snow, go to www.usborne-quicklinks.com

The eggs and chicks of black skimmers have mottled markings to help them blend in with beach sand and debris.

Snipe's stripes

A jack snipe uses the stripes on its body to help it to hide in the marshland where it lives. When it lands, it turns itself so that its stripes run in the same direction as the marsh grasses around it. This camouflage can be so successful that bird watchers sometimes tread on jack snipes by mistake.

If disturbed, the snipe flies off a little way, then drops down into the grass.

It crouches in the grass, where it will stay until the danger has passed.

It lines the stripes on its body up with the grasses around it for camouflage.

Feisty chicks

Fulmars leave their chicks alone while they go fishing at sea. The chicks might need to fight off attacks by skuas, eagles and gulls. They do this by spitting a smelly substance which destroys the waterproofing of the attacking bird's feathers. Even parent birds approach carefully until their chicks can recognize them.

If a fulmar chick is threatened, it spits a smelly orange substance at its attacker, over a distance of up to 1.5m (5ft).

Through the spring, more brown feathers appear as white ones are lost.

By the time summer arrives, all the ptarmigan's feathers are brown.

Winter wear

Ptarmigans live on the ground in tundra regions, which are covered in snow for half the year. They are in danger from eagles, owls and other birds of prey from the air, and foxes and coyotes on the ground. To make sure that they always blend into the landscape, ptarmigans change their plumage with the seasons.

In spring, the snow melts and the ptarmigan starts to lose its white feathers.

A ptarmigan in winter plumage blends into the snow.

CONFUSE OR DEFEND

All mammals have fur or hair on their bodies. It can help them defend themselves in a number of ways, usually by providing camouflage. Mammals have other ways, too, of outwitting attackers or making sure that they leave them alone.

Secret of the stripes

It may seem to us that zebras stand out against the green and yellow of their grassland home. But their main predators, lions, can only see in black and white. The zebra's stripy coat blends in with the way the grasses grow, providing excellent camouflage.

Zebras may use their striped coats to recognize each other. No two have the same pattern.

Herd on the run

Zebras' stripes can also confuse predators. Once a herd of zebras starts moving, their striped coats seem to merge together. This makes it very difficult for a predator such as a lion to pick out a single zebra to chase.

INTERNET LINK
For a link to a website where you can play a game to learn more about camouflage, go to www.usborne-quicklinks.com

Skunk spray

Skunks are small and can't move very fast, yet they have few enemies. If it feels threatened, the skunk moves into a warning position. This is an attacker's last chance to escape before the skunk lets off a spray of extremely smelly, acidic liquid. Most animals have learned to stay away from the skunk because of this.

If a skunk feels threatened, it raises its tail as a warning.

A skunk can spray up to 4.5m (15ft). The spray may temporarily blind an attacker.

Bony ball

Three-banded armadillos are covered in bony plates. By rolling into a ball, an armadillo becomes completely protected on the outside, with its soft belly tucked away inside. A rolled-up armadillo is safe from most predators. It's still vulnerable to jaguars, though, which might be able to crack open the hard shell.

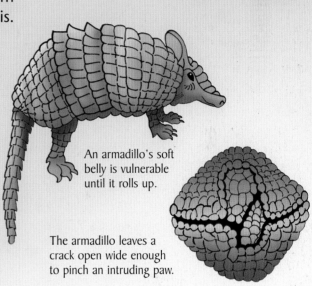

An armadillo's soft belly is vulnerable until it rolls up.

The armadillo leaves a crack open wide enough to pinch an intruding paw.

Hollow hairs

A polar bear looks white, but its hairs are actually clear tubes. These reflect light to make the bear look white or cream, so it blends in with its icy surroundings. The hollow hairs trap and magnify the Sun's rays, which helps to keep the bear warm. Surprisingly, the bear's skin is black, which also absorbs heat.

Heat from sunlight travels down the hollow hairs to the bear's black skin.

TRICKS AND MIMICS

Insects are often much smaller than their enemies, so they use camouflage, mimicry and tricks to avoid danger. Some have disguises that are realistic enough to frighten their attackers away.

Giant eyes

Caterpillars make juicy meals. If a puss moth caterpillar is threatened, it pulls in its head and inflates part of its body. The skin on this part has eyespot markings which look huge and scary when the segments bulge.

Beneath its waving tails, a puss moth caterpillar hides short, poisonous spines.

Moving thorns

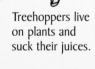

Treehoppers live on plants and suck their juices.

If disturbed, a treehopper jumps away with a snapping noise.

Treehoppers are insects with large, pointed outer cases. They look like thorns as they walk on the stems of plants. They have few enemies. Spiders can't bite through their hard covering and they are too spiny for birds to swallow.

To alarm predators, the caterpillar weaves its body from side to side like a snake.

56

Wrong end

If a butterfly is pecked by a bird, it is less damaging to be pecked on the edge of a wing than on its head. This is why a hairstreak butterfly has false antennae on the ends of its wings, which it uses to confuse predators.

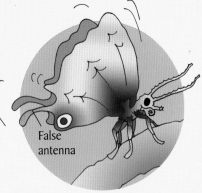

False antenna

A hairstreak butterfly lands and flaps its wings. This makes its false antennae move and look real.

A bird pecks the butterfly. It is confused by the false antennae and attacks the wrong end.

The butterfly flies away from danger but not in the direction that its attacker, confused by the false antennae, expects.

Owl eyes

Owl butterflies come out to find fruit at dusk. To avoid being eaten by small birds, they have owl-like markings. Small birds usually stay well away from anything that looks like an owl, in case they get eaten themselves. If a small bird does attack an owl butterfly, it usually goes for the eye markings on the wings and not the butterfly's body.

When its wings are outstretched, the owl butterfly's markings look like an owl's face.

Praying predator

A praying mantis uses its camouflage to hunt by stealth. It stands very still on a twig or branch, looking like a small twig itself, and waits for passing insect prey. It holds its lethal front legs together, and looks as if it is praying. This is how the insect got its name.

A praying mantis has sharp spikes on its front legs which it uses to grab its prey.

INTERNET LINKS
For links to websites where you can see butterflies that use camouflage, go to www.usborne-quicklinks.com

HELP OR HINDER

Some plants and animals live alongside each other and help each other out. But the relationship may be one-sided. A plant or animal that takes what it needs without giving anything in return is called a parasite.

Musical tree

Whistling thorn acacias provide homes for ants. At the bases of their thorns, there are hollow balls called ant galls. Ants live inside these.

If a tree is disturbed by a grazing animal, ants rush out of the ant galls and bite the animal, which sends it away.

Some ant galls are abandoned, leaving only hollow balls with holes. When the wind blows through them, it makes a whistling sound.

Acacias and ants

Bull's horn acacia trees provide the ants living inside their thorns with food and nectar. The food is in bundles on the ends of the leaves. Nectar comes in pots called nectaries at the bases of the leaves. In return, the ants protect the acacia. If an animal tries to eat the tree's leaves, ants swarm out and bite it.

INTERNET LINK
For a link to a website where you can watch how sloths move and find sloth photos and facts, go to www.usborne-quicklinks.com

Acacias grow food bundles on the ends of their leaves. The bundles have no use for the tree, except to attract ants, which eat them.

A food bundle

Hidden partners

Truffles are fungi that grow on tree roots underground. They take food from the tree but they also help it by releasing nutrients into the soil for it to use. Animals help truffles reproduce by carrying their spores to new places.

A truffle grows on the root of an oak tree. To grow, it takes nutrients from the tree and also from the soil.

A pig is attracted to the strong smell produced by the truffle. It digs it up and eats it.

Spores from the truffle pass out in the pig's droppings, in a new place. New truffles may grow.

Mobile home

Tiny plants called algae grow inside a sloth's hollow hairs, which makes its fur look green. This helps the sloth blend in with the forest greenery and so it is less likely to be spotted by predators. The algae benefit from the relationship by getting a place to live.

A sloth's green-tinged fur helps it to hide. The sloth keeps still and may look like part of the tree it is hanging from.

Space invasion

Not all relationships between living things are good for both. Strangler figs start off as small hitchhikers on larger trees. They use the tree for support, although they get nutrients from the ground through their own roots. But there is not enough light or water for two, and eventually the fig kills the other tree.

A strangler fig starts to grow from a seed dropped on a tree branch. The seed sprouts leaves and sends a shoot down to the ground.

The shoot reaches the ground and takes root. The fig gets water and nutrients from the soil, and wraps itself around the host tree.

The fig competes with its host for light, water and nutrients. It grows stronger and squeezes the tree to death. Only the fig is left.

59

OCEAN PARTNERS

Many sea creatures have relationships with others. In some partnerships, both sides benefit. In others, one partner slowly saps the other's strength and may even end up killing it.

Contract cleaning

Cleaner wrasse set up "cleaning stations" where other fish come to have pests and dead skin nibbled away. The wrasse clean between scales and inside the gills and mouths of bigger fish, and get a meal in the process. The bigger fish get a good clean, and in return for this, don't eat the wrasse.

Fish line up to visit a group of cleaner wrasse.

A cleaner wrasse may clean 2,500 clients in a day.

Poisonous protection

A clownfish can shelter among the poisonous tentacles of a sea anemone without getting stung. The fish coats itself in the anemone's own slime, tricking the anemone. The clownfish helps the anemone, too, by luring its own predators closer, for the anemone to trap and eat.

A clownfish must stay near the anemone and return to it carefully. If it loses its coating of slime, it can be stung like any other fish.

Team cleaning

Like cleaner wrasse, some shrimps set up cleaning stations. They wave their antennae to attract clients. Often the shrimps work in pairs. They pay special attention to the teeth of their clients. They have even been known to clean the teeth of human divers.

A cleaner shrimp picks scraps of food away from the razor-sharp teeth of a moray eel.

Intestine intruder

A sea cucumber can't defend itself against a parasitic pearlfish. Given the chance, the pearlfish wriggles tail-first inside the sea cucumber and snacks on its intestines. The cucumber doesn't benefit from the relationship but its internal organs do grow back after being eaten.

The pearlfish enters a chamber at the back of the sea cucumber's body, and lives inside.

The pearlfish may leave the sea cucumber to find other food, but it later returns to its host.

Flashing fish

A flashlight fish has pouches under its eyes, where light-producing bacteria live. The bacteria feed on the fish's blood. In return, they produce a bright light that can help the fish confuse an enemy. The fish turns the lights on and off by moving a flap of skin over each pouch.

If threatened by a hungry squid, the flashlight fish swims in one direction with its lights shining.

It then covers the light and rapidly changes direction, which confuses the squid.

INTERNET LINK
For a link to a website where you can take a virtual dive into a coral reef and see some clownfish, go to
www.usborne-quicklinks.com

SHARING SPACES

Reptiles are not naturally sociable creatures. But some form partnerships with other animals. They may share a nest, or hitch a ride. Crocodiles even get their teeth cleaned by small birds.

Plucky plover

Without its teeth, a crocodile would be unable to catch or eat food, and so it would die. But food scraps stuck between its teeth cause tooth decay, and parasitic leeches feed on its gums. Birds called plovers sometimes pick at the food scraps and parasites around a crocodile's teeth. They get an easy meal and the crocodile gets its teeth cleaned.

A plover picks at food scraps and pests between a crocodile's teeth.

Some plovers also pick irritating parasites off the crocodile's back.

The turtle's long claws help it hang onto the alligator's back.

Well-timed trip

Hungry alligators eat mainly fish but they may snap up any creatures that pass their way. A well-fed alligator is no threat to a turtle, though, and may even provide it with a free ride.

Borrowed burrow

Gopher tortoises dig large burrows to live in. They share their burrows with lots of different creatures – some friends, some foes. Up to 360 different species have been found in a burrow, including snakes, owls, armadillos, opossums, frogs and mice. Some of these help the tortoise keep its burrow clean.

A gopher tortoise digs a burrow that is as wide as the tortoise is long, so that it can turn around inside.

A gopher tortoise can block a pine snake intruder with its shell.

Gopher frogs eat insects that come into the burrow.

A visiting armadillo may eat the tortoise's eggs.

Gopher mice eat seeds that fall into the burrow.

Dangerous guest

Tuataras are lizard-like reptiles. They often share the burrows of sea birds called petrels. Both are night animals. The tuatara eats insects that live in the burrow but it may also eat the petrel's eggs, chicks, or even the petrel itself.

INTERNET LINK
For a link to a website about a partnership between a bird and a crocodile, go to
www.usborne-quicklinks.com

Both the tuatara and the petrel leave their shared burrow at night, to find food.

As the petrel flies in and out of the burrow, it stirs up insects, which the tuatara eats.

63

FINDING FOOD

Some birds hitch rides on other animals, or follow them, to find food. Sometimes the birds help the other creatures out in return, but not always.

Bird on bird

The picture shows a carmine bee-eater perching on the back of a kori bustard. As the heavy bustard tramples through grass, insects fly up to get out of its way. These are snapped up by the bee-eater. In return, the bee-eater warns the bustard of danger, as it will fly away if it spots predators.

In return for easy meals, the little bee-eater provides the bustard with an early-warning system. It will fly away if it spots a predator such as a lion, leopard or eagle.

Useful ants

Army ants work together in huge groups, and catch insects, frogs and even small mammals. Antbirds follow army ants, using them like a pack of hunting dogs to flush out prey. The most senior antbird follows the biggest army of ants, and so has the best chance of finding the most prey.

A column of army ants marches through a rainforest. An antbird runs and hops alongside them.

The army disturbs other insects and small animals. They must move, or risk being eaten by the ants.

The antbird snaps up some of the escaping insects with its slender beak.

Honey helpers

Honey guide birds eat honey, bee larvae and wax. They can't get into bees' nests on their own, though, so they seek the help of another creature – the honey badger.

Honey badgers eat almost anything they can find but they love honey most of all. They will happily follow a honey guide bird, knowing that it will lead them to a supply of honey. The badger breaks into the nest and the bird can eat, too. In this way, the two creatures help each other.

This honey guide bird has found a bees' nest in a tree. It will now look for a honey badger to help it open up the nest.

The honey badger follows the honey guide to the bees' nest. The badger rips open the nest with its sharp claws.

The badger feeds first, on honey. It leaves behind wax, bee larvae and some of the honey, for the honey guide.

Food on the move

Red-billed oxpeckers live near large animals on the African grasslands. They feed on the ticks, fleas and flies that live on cattle, elephants, giraffe, rhinos and antelopes. They also nibble at the animals' dead skin, mucus, saliva, sweat and especially their blood. Oxpeckers may help their host animals by getting rid of their parasites, but they will also nibble at an animal's wound, so it takes longer to heal.

INTERNET LINK
For a link to a website where you can see photographs of oxpecker birds and African animals, go to
www.usborne-quicklinks.com

A red-billed oxpecker eats parasites from places such as the inside of the ear, which this greater kudu can't reach with its own teeth.

65

MAMMALS' FRIENDS

Some mammals have relationships with plants or other animals that help them to survive. Their partners usually get something in return, like a share in the food or a place to live.

Useful bats

Many rainforest bats eat fruit. They pass the seeds of the fruit out in their droppings. For some fruit trees, this is the main way of spreading their seeds to new places.

Plants with pale flowers that come out at night tend to attract bats. The bats carry pollen on their fur from one plant to another, helping the plants to make seeds and reproduce.

This scary-looking bat only eats fruit. It uses its teeth to spear and grip the fruit.

Flowers that bloom at night are usually pale so they show up in the dark.

As a bat licks nectar from a night-blooming flower, pollen coats its furry body.

When it moves on to the next plant to feed, the pollen will rub off.

Useful ants

A pangolin's tough scales protect it, but also hide lice and other pests that the pangolin can't reach. Although a pangolin is an anteater, it may take a break from eating ants and instead let them clean it. The ants crawl in between its scales, eating the pests.

When the pangolin lifts its scales, ants can crawl underneath and eat lice and other pests.

Fishing together

Fishermen and river dolphins in the Irrawaddy River in Myanmar work together to increase their catch of fish. Their relationship has developed over hundreds of years. Both sides benefit from the partnership.

Dolphins herd a school of fish towards the fishing boats. Some stay back to stop fish from escaping.

When the fish are close enough, the dolphins signal to the fishermen to throw their nets by rolling over near the surface of the water.

The fishermen throw their nets. Any fish that aren't caught are easy prey for the dolphins.

Friendly bacteria

Some mammals, such as cattle, eat mainly leaves. But they can't digest a substance in the leaves, called cellulose, on their own. Bacteria living inside their digestive systems help them out. The bacteria break down the cellulose and turn it into substances that the animal can digest.

This is a microscopic view inside a cow's stomach. The red blobs are bacteria. The yellowish patch is undigested cellulose.

INTERNET LINK
For a link to a website where you can watch video clips about fruit bats and pangolins, go to
www.usborne-quicklinks.com

67

MEAL DEALS

Many kinds of insects go into partnerships with plants. In return for a supply of sweet nectar, the insects carry pollen from one plant to another. This enables the plants to make seeds and reproduce.

INTERNET LINK
For a link to a website with an interactive slide show about ants and aphids, go to
www.usborne-quicklinks.com

This bee has been drinking nectar from a flower. Fine pollen grains have rubbed off the flower onto the hairs on its body and legs.

Something for nothing

Unlike most bees, nectar-robbing bees are distinctly unhelpful to plants. They use their biting mouthparts to break into flowers and steal their nectar, without picking up and passing on the plant's pollen.

Once the nectar is gone, other creatures won't visit the plant. It doesn't receive pollen from another plant, so it can't make seeds.

A hummingbird sips nectar from a gilia plant's long, trumpet-shaped flowers. At the same time, it picks up and passes on pollen.

A nectar-robbing bee bites into a gilia flower. It drinks the nectar but doesn't pick up pollen. Hummingbirds won't visit, and pollinate, a robbed flower.

Live and let live

Yucca plants and yucca moths have to live together – in fact, they can't live without each other. This is because only yucca moths can pollinate yucca plants. In return, the moths get somewhere to lay their eggs – on the yuccas' flowers. When the eggs hatch, the caterpillars feed on the yucca plant's seeds. They can't survive on any other plant.

A female yucca moth visits different yucca plants' flowers, collecting pollen from each one. She rolls it together to form a ball, which she keeps under her chin.

The yucca moth stuffs pollen from the ball she has made into the female parts of other yuccas' flowers. They can then make seeds and reproduce.

Hidden flowers

A fig is not a real fruit, but is actually a fleshy bundle of flowers. These flowers can only be pollinated by a certain kind of female wasp, called a fig wasp. She wriggles inside the fig through a tiny hole, ripping her wings off in the process. She pollinates the flowers with pollen collected from a different fig, lays her eggs and then dies.

Egg-laying tube

This parasitic wasp lays its eggs in figs but doesn't burrow into or pollinate them. Instead, it pierces the fig with its long egg-laying tube.

A female fig wasp squeezes into a fig to lay her eggs. Young wasps will hatch and mate with each other.

The females then leave to find new figs to pollinate. The males are wingless and can never escape.

Fig wasp

Female fig wasp leaving

Bug farmers

Aphids suck plant juices and produce a kind of sweet, milky white liquid, made up of excess sugar. This is called honeydew and ants love it. Ants "farm" groups of aphids almost like people farm cows. They protect the aphids from other creatures in order to keep for themselves all the honeydew that the aphids produce.

An ant guards its flock of aphids. It feeds on the honeydew that they produce.

Aphids feed using piercing and sucking mouthparts. They multiply very quickly.

PLANT COMMUNITIES

The place where a plant grows naturally is called its habitat. Some plants and animals share the same habitat. They live together in communities.

Tank tenants

Tank bromeliads are plants that live perched high up on the branches of rainforest trees. They can't collect water from the ground so their waxy leaves form a cup, which collects a pool of rainwater. The tank also collects leaf litter from nearby trees, and gives a home to a collection of small animals.

A tank bromeliad shares its tank with visitors such as small frogs, insects and even a type of crab that only lives in bromeliads.

Tree frogs feast on insects that drop into the bromeliad's tank.

Two-in-one plants

A lichen is not just one plant but two – an alga and a fungus. They can't survive without each other. The fungus part provides a sturdy base for the alga to grow on, and soaks up water and food. In return, the alga uses sunlight to make food for itself and the fungus.

Lichens grow in many different shapes. Some, like this one, are flat and crust-like. Others are more leafy.

— Alga

— Fungus

— Rock

Lichens are slow-growing but are able to live in places where other plants can't, such as tree bark or the surface of rocks.

INTERNET LINK
For a link to a website where you can find out more about mangroves, go to www.usborne-quicklinks.com

Many-homed mangroves

Mangroves are trees which grow along coastlines and riverbanks. They have large bundles of roots to anchor themselves in the waterlogged, muddy ground. They provide a home for many creatures. Herons and sea birds roost in their branches. Mangrove crabs creep around on their trunks. Oysters, barnacles and sponges cling to partly-submerged roots. Fish lurk among the roots underwater.

Fish use the mangrove roots as a place to hide from predators that are too big to squeeze through the gaps.

Interlinked life

A rainforest is a huge ecosystem in which many thousands of plant and animal species live.

Communities of animals and plants living together are called an ecosystem. A rainforest is an ecosystem. A hedgerow is a much smaller example. Within ecosystems, plants and animals may depend on each other. The loss of a plant community from an ecosystem has an impact on the animals that live in it, endangering their survival.

Cutting down areas of rainforest kills the trees and plants that grew there. It would take centuries for many of these trees to grow back.

Animals that lived in the deforested area must find new homes or else they will die.

These mangroves are growing in a lake.

KEEPING IN TOUCH

Many fish gather in huge groups, called schools, as they move through the ocean. For some, this provides safety in numbers. Others get together to hunt. Members of a group need to be able to communicate with one another. They use body language, markings and sound to keep in touch.

Losing touch

A school of small fish moving together may look like a single large animal, and an individual fish is less likely to be eaten if it is surrounded by others. Hunting barracudas weave in and out of schools of smaller fish to break up their group and confuse them. A lone fish is easy prey for a barracuda, with its fiercely snapping teeth.

Barracudas can't open their mouths wide so they use sharp teeth to slash their prey.

One fish has become separated from the rest of the school. The barracuda singles this out.

Each fish has a sense organ called a lateral line, which lets it sense where other fish are. The lateral line runs along its body.

INTERNET LINKS
For links to websites where you can watch video clips of humpback whales and listen to their songs, go to www.usborne-quicklinks.com

72

Mood markings

Cuttlefish change their markings depending on their mood, which allows them to communicate with other cuttlefish. Most of the time, they blend into their surroundings. But to attract a mate, a male puts on a display of flickering patterns.

A cuttlefish's skin has cells filled with pigments, which expand and contract very quickly to make different patterns.

Long song

Humpback whales make moans, squeals and clicks to communicate with each other. But during the breeding season, males also sing complex songs to entice females and ward off rivals. A humpback whale's song can be heard by other whales up to 160km (100 miles) away. Humpback whales also show their emotions using dramatic body language.

Humpbacks leap out of the water, then fall back with a huge splash. This is called breaching.

They splash their long flippers against the surface of the water.

Versatile voices

Dolphins use sounds to communicate with each other, and to build up a picture of their surroundings. Each dolphin can make a unique whistle to identify itself to others. They can also make sounds to confuse fish and even knock them out.

Blowhole

Dolphins use echoes to sense their surroundings, including the position of fish schools nearby.

Dolphins make noises inside their blowholes to communicate with each other.

Huge tail fins, called flukes, make a very dramatic splash on the surface of the water.

CALLS AND SIGNALS

Reptiles and amphibians have some remarkable ways of communicating. They might use these to attract a mate, for instance, or to warn off enemies.

Croc conversations

Crocodiles, alligators, gharials and caimans are the noisiest reptiles. They make many different sounds, including distress calls, courtship bellows and defensive hisses. Alligators can bellow loudly. You can see how they do this on the right.

To threaten an enemy, a crocodile may combine a defensive hiss with a snap of its fearsome jaws.

As the alligator starts to bellow, the rumbling sounds make ripples on the surface of the water.

The alligator takes in air and raises its head and tail out of the water.

It waves its tail from side to side. It also starts to make the air inside its closed mouth vibrate.

INTERNET LINKS
For links to websites where you can listen to crocodiles and alligators, go to
www.usborne-quicklinks.com

Turn it up

Male frogs make loud calls. Large frogs make low-pitched croaks and small frogs make high-pitched squeaks. They call to attract a mate, to mark their territory or to show fear. One type of tree frog climbs inside hollow trees to amplify its call – like sitting inside a drum.

Some male frogs have throat pouches that help make their calls louder.

Touchy turtles

During the breeding season, a male painted turtle will try to charm a female into mating with him by gently caressing her cheeks with the long claws on his front legs. She will show if she is willing to mate with him by stroking his front legs in return.

A male swims up behind a female painted turtle and overtakes her.

He turns to face her. She keeps swimming, pushing him with her.

The male strokes the female's cheeks with his claws to see if she will mate.

Hooded warning

A cobra uses its hood to show anger or fear. The hood is made of skin stretched over ribs which can be raised to stand out around the snake's head. The cobra shows its hood to warn an animal that it may strike, with a deadly bite, if the animal doesn't escape quickly.

To scare an enemy into leaving it alone, a cobra makes its hood stand out, rears up and starts to sway and hiss.

If the enemy does not leave immediately after this warning, the snake will strike.

SHOWING OFF

Birds are great show-offs when it comes to attracting a mate. A male bird needs to prove to females that he is the best. He might get himself noticed by his bright feathers, or try to impress by performing a complicated dance to show how fit he is.

Interior design

Bowerbirds are the only creatures that use objects to impress the opposite sex – apart from humans. Male bowerbirds build dens, or bowers, out of twigs and grasses. They decorate them with leaves, flowers and feathers. They even use bottletops, plastic forks and other thrown-away things. When a female arrives at a bower, the male shows her his collection of objects. If she likes his display, they mate.

Satin bowerbirds paint the inside of their bower with the juice from blue berries.

They prefer to use blue objects to decorate their bowers.

This aracari's markings are made by pigments in its feathers.

Blue feathers shimmer in the light. This is called iridescence.

Fitness test

Many male birds use bright feathers to impress females. The fitter the bird, the brighter its plumage – and the fittest bird attracts the most mates.

Yellow, red, brown and black feathers contain pigments which a bird gets by eating certain fruits or seeds. Other feathers appear green or blue because of the way they reflect light.

Yellow feathers get their appearance from pigments in the bird's food.

Fashion shows

Male birds of paradise have vivid feathers, loud calls, and perform flamboyant dances, all in the hope of attracting a mate. Some birds even prepare a stage. They remove leaves from the area where they are going to dance, to increase their chances of being seen.

As a Raggiana bird of paradise displays its bright, velvety plumage, it also shrieks louder and louder.

Prince Rudolph birds of paradise hang upside-down to show off their feathers.

King of Saxony birds of paradise have two metallic-looking head feathers, 60cm (2ft) long, which wave as they bounce on branches.

Bowerbirds collect these feathers when birds shed them, to decorate their bowers.

INTERNET LINK
For a link to a website where you can learn some bird courtship steps, go to
www.usborne-quicklinks.com

FRIEND OR FOE

Many mammals live in groups. They defend each other against enemies, get rid of each others' parasites and form friendships and rivalries. They keep in touch using sounds and body language.

Each lemur in a group keeps its tail raised, to let the others know where it is at all times.

Touching teeth

Prairie dogs live in groups of thousands or even millions, called towns. Each town is divided into areas called wards, then into family groups called coteries. A coterie consists of a male, several females and their children. Prairie dogs touch teeth when they meet, to find out if they are from the same coterie.

The diagram below shows how a prairie dog town is divided into smaller groups.

Furry flag

Ring-tailed lemurs live in groups. They use their tails as markers to keep track of one another.

During the breeding season, males have scent battles. They rub their wrists against scent glands under their armpits, and coat their tails with the smelly substance. Then they wave their tails at each other in a threatening way, wafting the scent through the air.

When prairie dogs meet, it looks as if they kiss, but they are actually touching teeth.

Lemurs coat their tails with scent, then wave their tails to fan the scents at each other.

Grins and grimaces

The most important male mandrill in a group has bright blue and red patches on his face and body, which become even brighter when the mandrill is excited. Most mandrills, though, communicate using facial expressions and body language. But these expressions may not mean what you expect...

A yawn doesn't indicate boredom but is a warning – the mandrill is frustrated or about to attack.

A toothy grimace may look threatening but it is really a sign of friendship.

Groom mates

Chimpanzees spend a lot of time grooming each other to remove dead skin, dirt and parasites from each others' coats. Shared grooming also helps the chimpanzees to make friends, comfort each other and sort out fights. A chimpanzee who has been away for a few days will be greeted by his friends on his return with a long grooming session.

Chimps' fingers are good at picking pests and dirt from the hair and skin.

INTERNET LINK
For a link to a website where you can watch a short video about chimps and hear their call, go to www.usborne-quicklinks.com

TEAM WORK

Some insects live in large, well-organized groups called colonies. Each colony is controlled by a queen who is looked after by workers. She is the only insect in the colony to lay eggs. Every other insect has its own special tasks, to make sure that the colony runs smoothly.

These worker bees are tending the six-sided wax cells of the comb.

Honeypots on legs

Some honey ant workers, called "honeypots", store huge amounts of nectar inside their bodies. They stay inside the nest and other workers feed them. They gradually become filled with nectar. This sugary store can be shared between all the ants in the colony when food is scarce.

Honeypot ants can't leave the underground chambers where they live – they are too fat.

Hive of activity

Worker honeybees only live for about a month in the summer. They work so hard in that time that they die of exhaustion.

Their duties in the beehive change as they grow older. The oldest worker bees guard the hive and look for food.

Newly-hatched workers clean the hive's wax cells.

After a week, the workers start to care for the queen.

After two weeks, they start building new honeycomb.

Finding food

Honeybee scouts fly away from their hive to find food. When they return, they tell the rest of the colony what they have found by performing a dance, which the others bees follow by touch. Inside a beehive it is dark, and bees are almost deaf, so this is the best way to communicate.

To encourage other bees in the hive to go out and forage for food, scout bees perform a round dance. They circle in one direction or the other.

Scout bees perform the "waggle dance" to show how far away a source of food is. This is in the rough shape of a figure eight.

The middle of the eight is angled to show the direction of the food. As the bee walks along this line, it waggles. The more vigorous the waggling, the closer the food source is.

Egg-machine queen

Queen termites are little more than egg-laying machines. Some can lay up to 30,000 eggs every day. A queen can be up to 12cm (5in) long – much bigger than the other termites in the colony.

A queen termite is so big that she can't move. She relies on workers to feed her, clean her and care for her eggs.

INTERNET LINK
For a link to a website where you can watch video clips of honeybee waggle dances, go to
www.usborne-quicklinks.com

NEW PLANTS

Plants and fungi can reproduce in two ways. Asexual reproduction happens when part of a plant breaks away to form a miniature, identical plant. Sexual reproduction happens when two plant cells join together to make a seed, from which a new plant grows. This new plant is different from its parents.

Flying lanterns

Chinese lantern plants have red, papery wrappers around their seeds that work like kites. They catch the wind and carry the seeds far away from the parent plants. When the seeds land, they start to grow into new plants. The seed-wrappers look like Chinese paper lanterns, which is how the plant got its name.

This Chinese lantern has begun to disintegrate, leaving just a skeleton. You can see the seed inside.

Outside to inside

Some plants have both male and female reproductive parts. Pollen from the male part of one plant's flower must reach the female part of another plant's flower for them to reproduce sexually. Often the male parts stick out and are covered in pollen, which brushes off easily on passing insects, birds or bats.

Pistil

Stamen

This flame lily has prominent stamens, which are the male parts, tipped with pollen. This rubs off if an insect touches it.

Pistil

Pollen brushes off the insect onto the sticky pistil – the female part of another lily.

Seed

The pollen travels down the pistil, deep inside the flower. This is where the seeds form.

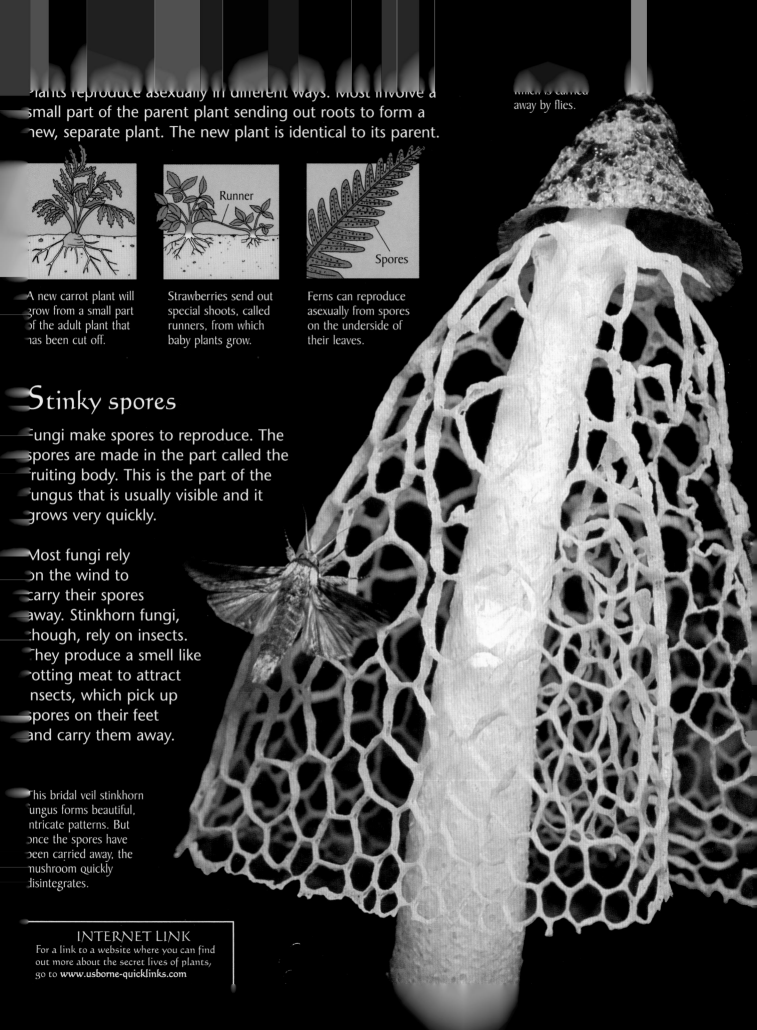

Plants reproduce asexually in different ways. Most involve a small part of the parent plant sending out roots to form a new, separate plant. The new plant is identical to its parent.

A new carrot plant will grow from a small part of the adult plant that has been cut off.

Strawberries send out special shoots, called runners, from which baby plants grow.

Runner

Ferns can reproduce asexually from spores on the underside of their leaves.

Spores

Stinky spores

Fungi make spores to reproduce. The spores are made in the part called the fruiting body. This is the part of the fungus that is usually visible and it grows very quickly.

Most fungi rely on the wind to carry their spores away. Stinkhorn fungi, though, rely on insects. They produce a smell like rotting meat to attract insects, which pick up spores on their feet and carry them away.

This bridal veil stinkhorn fungus forms beautiful, intricate patterns. But once the spores have been carried away, the mushroom quickly disintegrates.

which is carried away by flies.

INTERNET LINK
For a link to a website where you can find out more about the secret lives of plants, go to **www.usborne-quicklinks.com**

OCEAN OFFSPRING

Ocean creatures have fascinating solutions to the problems of finding a mate and bringing up young. But for some, parental responsibility ends as soon as the eggs are laid.

Mates for life

When a male anglerfish bumps into a female in the depths of the ocean, he clings on and never lets go. He receives all his food from her, through a shared blood supply. The arrangement means that she always has a male available to fertilize her eggs. This saves her from having to hunt for a mate in the darkness.

Fickle fish

Cuckoo wrasse, like some other species of fish, can change sex. All cuckoo wrasse are born female, but most change sex and become male as they grow older. If an old male wrasse in a mixed group dies, one of the females will change sex to replace him.

A female cuckoo wrasse

A male cuckoo wrasse

Males have different markings when they are courting.

Two male anglerfish are attached to this large female. She can carry as many as six males. At first, the male grips the female with his teeth. Eventually, his mouth becomes fused to her body.

84

This fish is hatching from its egg. The blood vessels carry food from the yolk to the fish.

Food supply

Most fish lay eggs which hatch outside their bodies. When the young fish first hatch, they are still attached to the sac of yolk which nourished them while they were inside the eggs. For a few days, this provides them with their own, ready-made food supply.

Deadly dash

Female loggerhead turtles always return to the beach where they hatched to lay their own eggs. Each turtle lays over 100 eggs and buries them in the sand. She lays so many because when the baby turtles hatch, they must rush across the sand to the sea. Many will be eaten by predators, such as sea birds, as they dash to safety.

After hatching, the baby turtles run as fast as they can to the sea.

Big baby

Whales are mammals, which means whale mothers feed their babies on their own milk. Newborn humpback whales are enormous – about 3.5m (12ft) long. They weigh up to two tons. This is as big as a large, well-loaded van. They stay with their mother for about a year.

A newborn whale calf drinks its mother's fat-rich milk.

After a year the whale calf has doubled in length.

INTERNET LINKS
For links to websites with movies of humpback whale calves and baby loggerhead turtles, go to www.usborne-quicklinks.com

PARENTAL CARE

Amphibians are creatures that spend time living in the water and on land, at different stages in their lives. Both reptiles and amphibians lay eggs. Some care for their young after they have hatched, feeding and protecting them.

Independent young

Most snakes lay soft, leathery eggs. They must keep them warm and moist for healthy young snakes to hatch. Some snake parents urinate on their eggs to stop them drying out too much. Many snakes look after their eggs before they hatch but leave their babies alone afterwards. A snake gets out of its egg using a sharp tooth on the tip of its snout, called an egg tooth, to slit the shell.

A python lays up to 100 eggs. She coils her body around them to keep them warm.

After three months, they hatch. The mother has lost half her body weight, and is so weak that she can't lay eggs for several years.

A baby snake may stay near its egg for several days after it first breaks the shell, until it feels safe enough to leave.

Backful of babies

Surinam toad mothers keep their eggs safe by carrying them around embedded in the skin of their backs. Baby toads develop completely inside the eggs, so that when they leave their mother, they are immediately able to look after themselves.

Baby toads develop inside the eggs. After three months, they emerge from the skin of their mother's back, looking like miniature adults. They are able to swim and eat right away.

A female Surinam toad lays her eggs on the male's tummy. He fertilizes the eggs and rubs them into her back. After a few days, they sink into the spongy skin, as shown above.

INTERNET LINK
For a link to a website with video clips of cobra eggs and babies, go to
www.usborne-quicklinks.com

Devoted mother

Baby crocodiles hatch from their eggs looking like small versions of their parents. They call to their mother as they are hatching, to let her know that they are there and need taking care of. She has already guarded her eggs constantly for two months, and continues to look after her young when they hatch. After a few weeks, her babies leave to fend for themselves and find places of their own to live.

This baby crocodile has just hatched.

Land and water

Some salamanders are amphibians. The young ones live underwater. The adults live on land but stay near water because they must lay their eggs in water. These salamanders have a four-stage life cycle, similar to other amphibians such as frogs, toads and newts.

A salamander lays its eggs in water. They are protected by a jelly-like substance which also nourishes them.

Larvae emerge from the eggs. They breathe with gills, and have small legs and long tails. They have teeth and feed on tiny insects.

The larvae develop lungs and can now breathe on land. They still spend most of their time in the water, though.

Adult salamanders walk on land but still have tails. They feed on worms and small insects, and return to water to lay eggs.

EGGS TO CHICKS

All birds lay eggs. An egg is like a womb outside the mother's body, protecting and feeding the chick inside. The advantage of laying eggs is that the mother doesn't have to carry the growing chicks in her body. She can fly around and search for food.

The life of an egg

An egg takes about a day to form inside a bird. The first part to form is the yolk, around the cell that will become the chick. The yolk is the food that will nourish the growing chick. The white forms around the yolk, then finally the shell forms and the egg is laid.

After several weeks, when the chick has used up the yolk and has grown to fill the shell, it is ready to hatch.

This chick is ready to hatch. It has used up all the yolk and fills the shell.

A cold start

Female emperor penguins lay their eggs in the middle of winter. They live on Antarctica, the coldest continent, and face a constant struggle to keep their eggs and chicks warm. If an egg touches the ice, the chick inside will quickly freeze to death.

A penguin keeps its chick warm under a flap of skin on its tummy.

A female lays one egg. She leaves it with the father. He balances the egg on his feet, under a warm flap of skin called a brood pouch.

After about 65 days, the female returns with food for the newly-hatched chick. She now takes care of the chick while the father finds food.

Keeping warm

All eggs must be kept warm, for healthy chicks to hatch. Birds use their body warmth to keep their eggs at the correct temperature, turning them regularly to heat them evenly. This is called incubation.

Most birds have brood patches. These are bare patches of skin where blood vessels run close to the surface. Some birds have a single, large brood patch. Others have separate patches for each egg.

Geese pluck feathers from their chest to make one large brood patch. They save the feathers and use them to line their nest.

Blue-footed boobies keep their eggs warm on their large, webbed feet. When the chicks are nearly able to fly, the parents leave them.

INTERNET LINK
For a link to a website where you can see a chick hatch and try an egg game, go to www.usborne-quicklinks.com

Putting in the time

European robins are helpless when they first hatch. The chicks are tiny, blind and can't fly. They eat almost constantly – parent birds may make hundreds of trips a day to find food for their chicks.

Eggs that hatch quickly tend to produce more helpless chicks. Eggs that need a long incubation before they hatch tend to result in chicks which can look after themselves almost immediately. Either way, eggs and chicks take up a lot of parents' time.

A robin chick signals that it needs to be fed by opening its mouth wide. The inside of the mouth is bright orange or red to show up inside the murky nest.

MAMMALS' MILK

Mammals spend more time than any other animals caring for their young. Mammal mothers feed their babies on milk, which they make inside their bodies. The babies depend on this until they can eat other food. They may spend months or years with their mothers.

Long-term love

After a nine-month pregnancy, a female orang-utan gives birth to one baby. The baby drinks its mother's milk until it is six or seven years old. Even after the young orang-utan has stopped drinking milk, it stays in its mother's care for another few years. Finally, at the age of about ten, it leaves its mother and can fend for itself.

For the first four months of an orang-utan's life, it clings to its mother's front and feeds on her milk.

After four months, the baby begins to eat soft fruit, given to it by its mother. It still drinks milk as well.

Orang-utans usually live alone, but males and females come together to mate. After that, the female will take care of their baby for up to ten years.

90

Fast food

When Weddell seals are born, they must build up a layer of fat quickly to survive the Antarctic cold. To do this, they drink their mother's fatty milk. Weddell seals' milk is about 60% fat (compared to cows' milk, which is about 4% fat). Within a week, a pup is fat enough to take to the water. It doubles its weight in ten days.

A Weddell seal pup is born small and slim, in contrast to its fat mother. She is as round as a barrel. The pup begins to suckle right away.

The newborn pup feeds constantly. After a month, the pup is plump and well-fed but its mother is skinny and exhausted.

Eggs and milk

Platypuses belong to an odd group of mammals called monotremes, which are egg-laying mammals. Monotremes have many mammal-like features, such as furry bodies and the ability to feed their young with milk. They also have reptile-like features, though, such as laying leathery eggs instead of giving birth to live young.

When the eggs hatch, the babies drink milk. It oozes out of two patches of skin on the mother's tummy.

A female platypus lays her eggs in an underground nest and incubates them on her tummy, with her tail curled around them.

INTERNET LINK
For a link to a website where you can watch video clips of mammal babies, go to www.usborne-quicklinks.com

First journey

Wallabies are mammals with pouches, called marsupials. A wallaby gives birth to her baby, or joey, after it has spent only 28 days in her womb. It is tiny and helpless, so it crawls up her fur from the birth opening to find her pouch, where it stays for the next few months.

When it is bigger, it leaves the pouch for short periods. After about a year, the joey stops drinking its mother's milk and leaves the pouch for good.

A joey crawls up to the mother's pouch from her birth opening. It is blind and about the size of a rice grain.

Inside the pouch, the joey sucks milk from its mother's nipple.

Six months after birth, a joey's weight has increased by about 2,000 times.

NEW GENERATIONS

Some insects go through amazing changes during their development from egg to adult. In the middle stages, their bodies may not resemble the adult insect at all.

INTERNET LINK
For a link to a website all about butterflies and their life cycles, go to www.usborne-quicklinks.com

This photo has been adapted to show three stages of a butterfly's life cycle at once.

A newly-emerged swallowtail butterfly waits for blood to flow into its wings before it can fly away.

Changing shape

A butterfly goes through four stages during its life cycle.

The chrysalis looks a little like a dead leaf. This protects it from being eaten.

First, it hatches from an egg into a caterpillar.

The chrysalis splits open and a butterfly emerges, ready to mate and lay eggs.

The caterpillar eats until it is plump and almost bursting.

The caterpillar's body hardens into a chrysalis. Its body is rearranged inside to make a butterfly.

A swallowtail caterpillar looks nothing like the butterfly it will turn into.

Baby boom

Aphids have a complicated life cycle which involves sex change and having babies without mating. This allows them to reproduce very quickly during the summer. If all the aphids descended from a single female in one summer were lined up end to end, they would stretch more than four times around the Earth.

This female aphid is giving birth to a live daughter.

Female aphids hatch from eggs on a host plant. They give birth to daughters which soon have their own babies, without mating.

The aphid population explodes. The aphids feed on the host plant. They may weaken or even kill the plant.

Some aphids grow wings and fly to different plants to feed. But as summer ends, aphids return to their original plant species.

At the end of the summer, some aphids become male. They mate with the females, who lay eggs, which will form the next generation.

Shedding skin

Young locusts, called nymphs, grow quickly when it is warm. Their skin doesn't grow with them, though. As they get bigger, they shed their skin several times. Locusts have a three-stage life cycle – egg, nymph and adult.

A female locust digs a hole to lay her eggs in. Nymphs hatch, looking like tiny, wingless adults.

A nymph eats constantly and grows quickly. It sheds its skin several times before becoming an adult.

By the time it is an adult, the locust has wings and is ready to fly away and mate.

PLANT INTRUDERS

Some plants don't grow in soil in the usual way. Instead, they grow on other plants. This is because they can't make enough – or any – food for themselves, so they steal it from a plant that can. Plants that do this are called parasitic plants.

Fleeting flower

The biggest flower in the world is the rafflesia. A single flower may measure up to 1m (36in) across. Rafflesia is a parasitic plant which has no stem, roots or leaves of its own. It feeds by breaking into the roots of a tropical vine. It spends most of its life hidden underground and only flowers for a short time.

Vine's root

A rafflesia seed lands on the ground near the roots of a tetrastigma vine. The seed sends tiny threads into the vine's roots to feed itself.

Vine's root

After about 18 months, the rafflesia forms a bud on the ground near the base of the vine. It grows up to 16cm (6in) across.

INTERNET LINK
For a link to a website where you can watch a rafflesia bloom, go to www.usborne-quicklinks.com

Nine months after a bud forms, it flowers. The flower has thick, fleshy petals and gives off a strong smell which attracts flies to pollinate it. After a few days, it rots into a black slime.

Piggy back plant

Mistletoe grows on tree branches. It uses its own green leaves to make food but also saps nutrients from its host. Many mistletoe plants may grow on a single tree. Mistletoe doesn't usually kill the tree, though, because if the tree dies, the mistletoe will die too.

A mistletoe seed, dropped by a bird, takes root on a branch and starts to grow.

The plant sends suckers into the tree's bark to sap extra nutrients. It also makes its own food using sunlight.

Birds eat the mistletoe's berries, which contain its seeds. The seeds pass out in the birds' droppings. Some land on new tree branches and grow there.

Dark invaders

Squawroots have no green leaves, and can't make their own food using sunlight. Instead, they break into the roots of oak or beech trees to steal their nutrients. Because they don't need sunlight to grow, they can survive in complete shade, or even when buried by leaves fallen from their host tree.

These squawroots are covered in flower buds and have small, scaly, brown leaves.

Squawroots grow in North America. They are often eaten by hungry bears that have woken from their winter sleep.

PLACES TO STAY

The ocean floor is a varied seascape and there are swift currents up near the surface. Below and above, creatures find places to hide and ingenious ways to stop themselves being swept away.

Coral caves

Coral reefs are full of cracks and crevices, which make good hiding places for fish such as moray eels. These lurk in caves during the day with only their heads poking out, snapping at fish that swim by. Their skin blends in with the coral. At night they come out of hiding to hunt for prey in the dark.

This moray eel is lying in wait with its jaws gaping, ready to snap up passing fish. Even the inside of its mouth is camouflaged against its hiding place.

INTERNET LINK
For a link to a website with a sea otter webcam and other otter information, go to www.usborne-quicklinks.com

Night anchor

Sea otters have an original way to stop themselves drifting away from their family when they go to sleep. They wrap themselves up in long ribbons of a seaweed called kelp. Sea otters live in large family groups, hunting by day for sea urchins, which they crack open with rocks. They never leave the water.

Kelp grows up from the sea bed in long strips, which the otter wraps around its body.

Lawn of eels

Garden eels live in colonies on the sea floor. They bury their back ends in the sand and let their heads drift. They feed on tiny ocean creatures, called plankton, that float by on the gentle currents.

A moray eel is stealthy enough to make a surprise attack on a colony of garden eels.

A colony of garden eels resembles an underwater lawn, swaying in the ocean currents.

If danger threatens, a garden eel can retreat into its burrow with lightning speed.

Coral cities

Coral polyps are tiny creatures that build hard skeletons underneath themselves. They can withdraw into their skeletons but spend most of their time outside, catching plankton to eat in their waving tentacles.

Many types of coral polyps live close together in their millions and form reefs. But some, like the cup coral below, live alone.

This cup coral has caught a small fish in its stinging tentacles. Its skeleton base is very large, at around 1cm (0.5in) across.

FITTING IN ANYWHERE

Most animals live mainly on land or in water and their bodies are adapted accordingly. Amphibians, though, are equally at home in either place.

Water and land

Amphibians such as frogs, toads, newts and some salamanders, have lungs and must breathe air. But they also take in oxygen through their moist skins, both from the air while they are on land, and underwater. They have powerful legs and are superb swimmers. This gives them advantages underwater when it comes to escaping predators and hunting for food.

If a frog is threatened by a land predator, it dives into the water to escape. It has webbed feet for serious swimming.

Frogs feed on water creatures like insect larvae and fish. If food in the water is scarce, they hop back onto land for a meal of insects, spiders, snails and worms.

This amphibian, called a fire-bellied newt, spends most of its time in the water. It comes onto land to rest or to bask in the sun.

This picture shows a close-up view of a hellbender's wrinkled skin.

Streambed salamander

Hellbender salamanders make their homes underwater, at the bottoms of rivers. Their bodies are flattened so currents rush over them, instead of sweeping them away. They live under rocks, blending into the background and hunting by stealth. They eat anything they can swallow.

A hellbender breathes through its skin, which is wrinkled to give a greater surface area.

All at sea

Sea snakes are reptiles, like land snakes, but they have some special features that allow them to spend their entire lives at sea. Their bodies are slightly flattened and they have paddle-shaped tails to help them swim. Sea snakes can dive up to 100m (110yd) to search for food. But usually they stay in shallower water, so that they can easily come to the surface to breathe.

A sea snake has special valves over its nostrils, that close to keep the water out when it is diving.

A sea snake can take in enough air to stay underwater for about two hours between breaths.

One long lung, shown in yellow, runs the entire length of a sea snake's body.

INTERNET LINK
For a link to a website where you can find out about amphibians, with video clips and photo galleries, go to www.usborne-quicklinks.com

Tree house

Tree snakes have long, thin bodies and wide belly scales to grip tree trunks. All tree snakes have extremely strong muscles, which they use to help them climb. Some have backbones and muscles strong enough to support half their body, anchored by the other half wrapped around a branch. This allows them to reach for prey across slender, widely-spaced branches.

To climb a thin tree, a tree snake wraps its back end around the trunk and reaches higher up the tree with its head.

When its front end has managed to get a good grip, the tree snake pulls up the back part of its body to follow.

To climb a tree that is too wide to wrap itself around, a tree snake slithers up the trunk as if it were on the ground, gripping with its wide belly scales.

NEST BUILDING

Birds build nests in places where their eggs and chicks will be safe from predators and the hazards of the environment. Some nests hide their occupants. Others are built high up, to keep eggs and chicks out of harm's way.

Joint effort

Great blue herons nest in colonies at the tops of trees or on cliff ledges. Each male heron chooses a nest site and defends it from other males. He might build a new nest from scratch or repair an existing one.

The male heron searches for sticks and twigs. He brings them to the female and she builds the nest.

A heron pair takes up to a week to make a nest solid enough for the female to lay her eggs. They continue to add sticks after the eggs hatch, to strengthen it.

A weaver bird starts a nest by tying a strip of grass in a knot around a branch. It then adds to it gradually.

INTERNET LINK
For a link to a website where you can watch birds' nests via webcams, go to
www.usborne-quicklinks.com

Hidden contents

Weaver birds build intricately woven nests. They are made of grasses, which the male bird tears into strips, then knots and weaves together using his beak and claws. The nest has a downward-facing entrance, which helps protect the mother and chicks from hawks and snakes. But some hawks feel the nests with their feet, to find out if there are eggs or chicks inside.

Tucked-up safe

African penguins dig nest burrows. They hollow them out of soil, or piles of other birds' droppings. The burrows protect their eggs and chicks from predators, and also shelter them from the hot sun. The main threat to the chicks is from a burrow collapsing.

Fairy feet

Fairy terns don't build a nest at all. They just perch their egg on a tree stump or piece of driftwood, in a dent on a tree branch, or even in the fork where two branches meet. The chick hatches complete with oversized feet that can grip its perch, however precarious.

This fairy tern chick was hatched in a high place. It hangs on tight with its large feet.

It takes about two weeks for a penguin to make a burrow. Instead, they may shelter in burrows dug by other birds or animals.

101

A PLACE TO SLEEP

Mammals need safe places to sleep. Not many can risk sleeping out in the open, especially young ones. Most make temporary or permanent shelters from materials they find nearby.

Different dens

For most of the year, adult foxes sleep and take shelter wherever they can. This might be in a hollow tree, under a rock or even curled up in a drainpipe. They rest during the day and come out at night to hunt.

When they have a family, though, some foxes dig an underground den. The female stays inside the den, guarding the pups, while her partner hunts for food.

These foxes are using a rocky crevice as a temporary den to shelter in.

A fox's underground den may have many chambers and several entrances.

Camping out

Some rainforest bats make their own safe places to sleep, in tents made from leaves. The bats chew along leaf veins to make folds in a leaf, then sleep inside the tent this creates. A leaf tent can last for up to a year.

A bat starts to make a leaf tent. It bites holes in the leaf with its teeth to make it droop.

The two sides of the leaf form a tent. Up to 15 bats might roost under a single banana leaf tent.

Most bats sleep in a tent made out of their own folded wings.

Lazy life

Koalas live in and feed on eucalyptus trees. But leaves don't provide much energy so they spend about 80% of their time asleep, curled up in the fork of a branch.

When they are awake, they are either feeding or just sitting still. They only come down to the ground to move to a new tree.

INTERNET LINK
For a link to a website where you can watch beavers build a lodge, go to www.usborne-quicklinks.com

A koala sleeps, clinging onto a tree branch with its sharp claws.

Secret entrance

Beavers live in families consisting of two parents and their young, in a home called a lodge. The only way to get into the lodge is by swimming underwater to reach its entrance. This means that the family can sleep safely there, protected from predators such as wolves and bears.

Beavers use their long front teeth to chop down trees.

They use wood and mud to dam streams and form lakes.

The lodge is a pile of sticks and branches in the middle of the lake.

INSECT PALACES

Many kinds of insects build homes using materials they can find easily, such as wood or mud. Some make an amazing team effort to build enormous structures for their colony, thousands of times larger than the insects themselves.

Massive mound

Termites build taller structures than any creature apart from humans. Their huge mounds are ventilation shafts, which provide fresh air for the underground nests beneath. Some mounds are over 12m (39ft) high.

Termite mounds are made of mud and saliva. Some are shaped like umbrellas to shed rain water.

Little lodgers

Slender ants live inside the thorns of acacia trees. This provides them with shelter and food. In return, the ants sting animals that might try to eat the tree. Slender ants share their thorny home with scale insects. These suck the plant's juices and make a sweet substance, called honeydew, which the ants feed on.

Scale insect

Cocoon containing a developing ant larva

Ant

Here you can see slender ants, ant larvae and scale insects covered in sticky, white honeydew.

INTERNET LINK
For a link to a website where you can explore a honeybee hive and play a termite game, go to www.usborne-quicklinks.com

This ant is carrying
a cocoon to a different
part of the nest.

Self-build colony

A paper wasp queen starts to build
her nest in spring, after spending
the winter tucked up in a crack or
crevice. The nest houses her
new colony of female workers.
It only lasts for one summer.
She then dies. The next
year, a new queen will
start another nest.

The young wasps
that emerge will
form a new colony.

She lays an egg in each
cell. Larvae will hatch
and develop in the cells.

The queen wasp builds a
nest of wood and saliva,
made of six-sided cells.

Leaf home

Leaf-mining caterpillars
live inside leaves, eating
them from the inside. This is
the juiciest part of a leaf and the
easiest to digest. The leaves also protect
the growing caterpillars from predators
and the weather. When the caterpillars
change into moths, they fly away.

This leaf is scarred with curving
patterns where caterpillars have
eaten tunnels inside it.

105

A TOUGH LIFE

Some plants have special features that allow them to grow in places that are too hot, dry or cold for other plants. Still, even these plants can be damaged or killed by really unusual weather conditions.

Some deserts have so little rain that these flowers may only bloom every five years.

Reacting to rain

Cacti have fleshy stems that expand to store water after any rain in the desert. Their roots collect water from near the surface of the ground, before it drains away. They flower after rain, producing seeds for the next generation before drought sets in again.

Cactus spines are actually very thin leaves, with a small surface area so they don't lose much moisture.

Seed survival

Desert soil is full of seeds. There may be hundreds in a handful. Some flower within hours of beginning to grow after rain. The blooms last a few days, then the plants die. Some deserts are so dry that there may be many years between flowerings – but the seeds can survive the wait.

Part-time leaves

Ocotillo plants survive in very dry conditions by only coming into leaf when there has been heavy rain. Their stems have green parts that can make food for the plant using sunlight, so it does not need to have leaves all the time – they would only provide more area for water loss.

For most of the year, an ocotillo looks like a bunch of dead sticks. One plant has up to 75 stems, with spines along their length.

Immediately after rain, the ocotillo bursts into leaf. The fleshy leaves grow in bunches. The plant also flowers every year.

The ocotillo's flowers are red and tube-shaped. Their shape means they can only be pollinated by hummingbirds.

Branching out

Joshua trees are shaped by the weather. If the temperature in the desert drops below freezing, flowers form at the growing tips of the plant. After flowering, the plant branches off in a new direction. If there are no flowers, no branches form and the plant grows straight up.

Joshua trees grow slowly – about 2cm (1in) per year. A single plant lives for around 200 years, on average, but some are up to 1,000 years old.

Cold start

A tiny alpine snowbell starts growing while there is still snow covering the ground. This means it is ready to push its flowers into the open as soon as the snow starts to melt. This in turn means that its flowers can produce seeds before larger plants grow and crowd it.

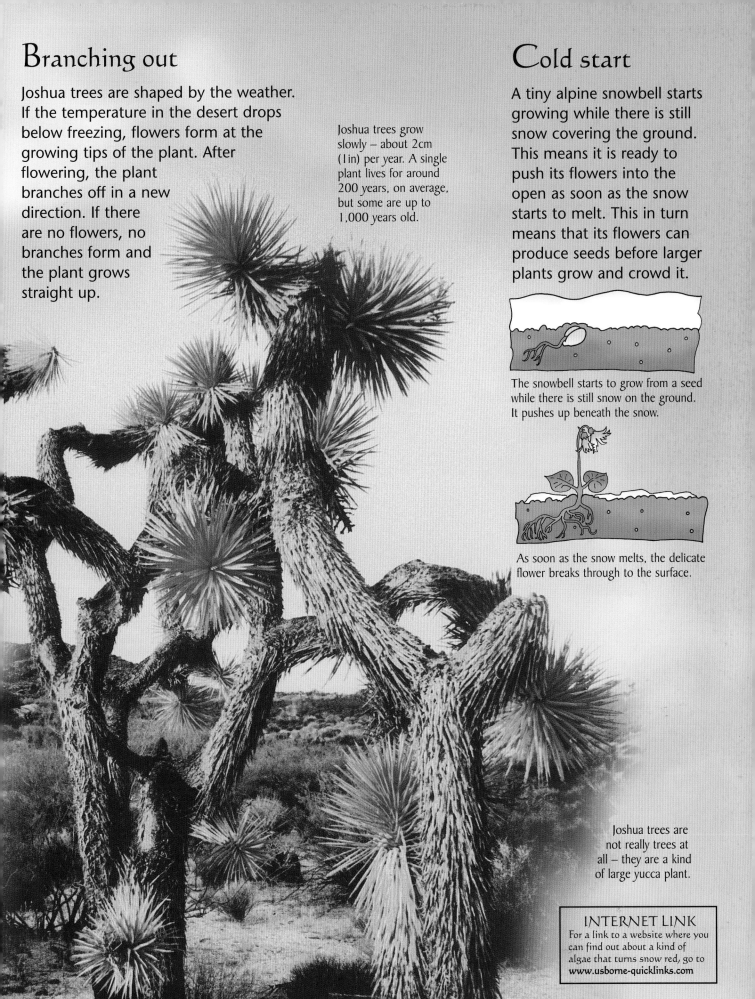

The snowbell starts to grow from a seed while there is still snow on the ground. It pushes up beneath the snow.

As soon as the snow melts, the delicate flower breaks through to the surface.

Joshua trees are not really trees at all – they are a kind of large yucca plant.

INTERNET LINK
For a link to a website where you can find out about a kind of algae that turns snow red, go to www.usborne-quicklinks.com

107

SEA MONSTERS

The deep sea is home to some weird, wonderful and terrifying creatures. They have found ways to cope with their surroundings – the temperature, the changing pressure and the almost complete lack of light to see by.

Looking up

Hatchet fish skulk around in deep waters, shrouded in darkness. They have upturned eyes to spot smaller fish silhouetted above, and attack unexpectedly, from below. A hatchet fish has lights which can be dimmed or brightened to blend in with light from above, making it hard to see from deeper down in the depths.

A hatchet fish has lights along its bottom edge.

The hatchet fish's mouth is upturned, for scooping up prey. The fish is only small, about 3–5cm (1–2in) long.

Monster squid

A real deep-sea monster is the giant squid. Scientists think they grow as long as 30m (100ft) – and possibly even longer. None, though, have ever been seen alive in their natural habitat. Instead, gruesome clues to their existence turn up occasionally, like the body of one washed ashore, or the sucker-scarred skin of a sperm whale.

Giant squids live in the murky depths. Their bodies function best in cold water.

Sperm whales have been found with giant squid sucker wounds on their skin.

Vicious viperfish

A viperfish is a deep-sea predator, with long, needle-like teeth. Its prey can't see it coming – the ocean depths are too dark. It is designed to be able to swallow anything it comes across. The fish's lower jaw is hinged, so it can swallow large victims. Most of its organs are near the head. The rest of its body is just an expandable tube, for digesting all sorts of prey.

The viperfish's bottom teeth are so large that they don't fit in its mouth. Its jaws are very strong so it can grip its victims before swallowing them.

This viperfish may look terrifying, but it is only 25cm (10in) long.

INTERNET LINK
For a link to a website where you can take a virtual dive into the deep and see videos of the fish, go to
www.usborne-quicklinks.com

Hot home

Where deep-sea water seeps into a crack or vent in the ocean floor, it is heated by red-hot rocks. The water near the vent is cold – around 2°C (36°F) – but the water in the vent is very hot – around 375°C (707°F). Some creatures can survive these extreme temperatures.

Hot, chemical-filled water gushes out of a vent, looking like a plume of black smoke. Tubeworms, clams and crabs cluster around the opening.

Tubeworms have feathery tops that absorb minerals from the water. Bacteria use these minerals to make food for the tubeworm. In return, the bacteria get a safe place to live, near the vent.

Some kinds of ghostly white crabs are able to survive in the extreme temperatures near the vent. They nibble on the tubeworms.

COOK OR CHILL

A few reptiles and amphibians are able to stand extreme heat or cold. Some can even survive droughts which would dry out and kill other creatures.

A lizard rests on its belly to cool all four feet.

Too hot to handle

Frogs, like other amphibians, need to stay moist to survive. During hot, dry months, an Australian water-holding frog burrows into the ground and goes to sleep. This is called aestivation. It is similar to hibernation, which means sleeping through the coldest months of the year.

INTERNET LINK
For a link to a website with amazing thermal images of warm and cold-blooded creatures, go to www.usborne-quicklinks.com

This water-holding frog is at the bottom of a stream – an ideal, moist environment for an amphibian.

Inside its burrow, a water-holding frog curls up inside a cocoon made of its own shed skin. This seals water near its body.

When there is heavy rain, water seeps through the ground and reaches the frog's burrow. The frog wakes up.

The frog peels the skin cocoon off with its legs and pulls it over its head. The frog stuffs the cocoon in its mouth and eats it.

110

Keeping cool

Surface temperatures in the desert can reach 65°C (150°F). Fringe-toed lizards lift each foot in turn to cool them down enough to walk on them. If it still feels too hot, the lizard dives below the surface of the sand, where it can stay for up to 24 hours.

Sand diving is also how the lizard escapes from predators. But if it rains while the lizard is above ground, the sand gets too hard for the lizard to burrow, and it is trapped.

The lizard lifts each foot in turn to cool them.

Keeping it in

Crocodiles bask in the sun to keep warm but the heat could also dry them out. To avoid this, their skins are almost waterproof, to seal water in. The large scales on a crocodile's back (which receives more sun than its belly) form a completely waterproof barrier. The belly scales are smaller and form a flexible, less waterproof surface which allows the crocodile to move.

The large scales on a crocodile's back are like shields, sealing water in. The belly scales don't need to provide as much protection from the sun, as they are shaded most of the time.

Deep freeze

A few reptiles and amphibians, including some frogs, toads and turtles, can survive cold winter temperatures by hibernating. Some burrow below the level of frost in the ground or stay underwater. Others, like the wood frog, can cope with being partly frozen. Up to one-third of the wood frog's body fluid freezes solid, but its vital organs stay working all winter to keep it alive.

A crocodile basks in the sun. It may get very hot but it never sweats, as this would dry its body out.

As cold weather approaches, the wood frog burrows into the leaf litter on the forest floor.

The top layers of ground freeze during winter and the frog freezes with them. Its body systems slow down while it hibernates.

BIRD EXTREMES

Birds have many special features that help them cope with everyday life. Some have more extreme conditions to cope with than others – dealing with intense cold, for instance, or living in permanent darkness.

An Arctic tern has long wings but very short legs, as it spends so much of its time in the air.

Extremely far

Arctic terns spend the brief Arctic summer breeding and raising young. Then they fly south to the Antarctic, to feast on krill in the Southern Ocean. Like many migrating birds, they follow the ocean winds and rarely touch down on land. In a year, each tern completes an average round trip of 35,000km (22,000 miles).

Arctic

Antarctic

Arctic terns make the longest yearly migration of any bird.

INTERNET LINK
For a link to a website with video clips of penguins, go to www.usborne-quicklinks.com

Penguin chicks huddle together to fight the cold. They take turns standing near the edge of the group.

Extremely cold

Emperor penguin chicks are born in winter and are well able to cope with the Antarctic cold. They have thick, downy coats and are extremely fat. For extra warmth, the chicks huddle together in large groups called crèches, while their parents go fishing. By the time the chicks take their first swim, the weather is warmer. It's not so far to walk to the sea, either, since as sea ice melts, the edge of the water creeps closer.

Extremely fast

The fastest flying bird on record is the peregrine falcon. It uses gravity to help it make dizzyingly fast dives, called stoops, and knock its prey out of the sky. It can reach speeds of over 160kph (100mph). Incredibly, it is still able to steer at this speed. If it misses the first time, it can pull up and attack from beneath. A human fighter pilot changing direction as suddenly as this would probably lose consciousness.

A falcon climbs above a pigeon in the air, then goes into a fast dive.

The falcon hits the pigeon so hard that it kills it immediately.

Extremely dark

During the day, oilbirds roost deep inside pitch dark caves. They make loud clicks and listen to the echoes bouncing off objects around them to find their way.

At night, they leave their caves and use their keen sense of smell to find ripe fruit trees. They also have excellent vision to help them fly through the dark forests.

Navigation by listening to echoes is called echo location. Other creatures that use it include dolphins and bats.

HEATING AND COOLING

Mammals' bodies stay at a steady temperature but they can still feel the cold or heat. They have different ways of dealing with harsh climates.

Thermostat ears

Black-tailed jackrabbits live in deserts, where temperatures swing between extremes of hot and cold. At night, the temperature drops, and the jackrabbit's long ears lie along its back to save heat and keep its body warm. During the hot, sunny days, its ears stick straight up, to give off heat.

A jackrabbit's ears keep the chill off its body at night. Folding them flat helps keep heat from escaping.

The ears are full of blood vessels. Wind passing across them cools the blood flowing close to the surface.

In hot water

Japanese macaques live on mountains that are covered in snow and ice during winter, when the temperature drops as low as -10°C (14°F). They have thick fur and hug each other to keep warm. A few lucky macaques live near natural hot springs. The macaques bathe in the steamy, volcanic pools to keep warm.

Outside the warmth of the pool, the macaques' fur quickly gets covered in snow and ice.

Furry feet

Snowshoe hares have very long, furry feet, which help to keep them from sinking in deep snow. Even the sides of the feet and the gaps between the toes are covered in fur. If the snow is very soft and powdery, a hare will spread all four toes on each back foot, to make a larger surface area.

The snowshoe hare is only white during winter. When spring arrives and the snow melts, its coat begins to turn brown for better camouflage.

INTERNET LINK
For a link to a website with a webcam showing snow monkeys bathing in a hot pool, go to www.usborne-quicklinks.com

Hay hoarders

Pikas live in places where the summers are warm but the winters are icy, with little food. In summer, they gather grass and pile it under sheltered rocks, where air dries it out. A pika gathers a big enough food supply to last it through the coming winter.

Each pika makes its own haystack and guards it fiercely.

Big dippers

Rhinos live in hot, grassland areas, with little shade from the burning midday sun. They search for food early in the day when it is cooler. Later on, they spend their time wallowing in mud. This cools the rhinos down and the mud helps to keep the sun off their skin. It also protects them from biting insects.

Rhinos prefer to forage for grasses, fruit and leaves during the early morning, before the day becomes too hot.

During the afternoon, rhinos go to streams or swamps, where they spend hours wallowing in mud to keep cool.

TINY PIONEERS

Insects and other creepy-crawlies can live in places where no other animals are able to survive. They also live in great numbers wherever there are people, feeding on the scraps we leave behind.

Sturdy springtails

Springtails are microscopic creatures that are able to survive Antarctica's freezing temperatures. They live in places where the ground is not usually covered in ice, such as inland valleys. A special liquid in their blood prevents their body fluids from freezing.

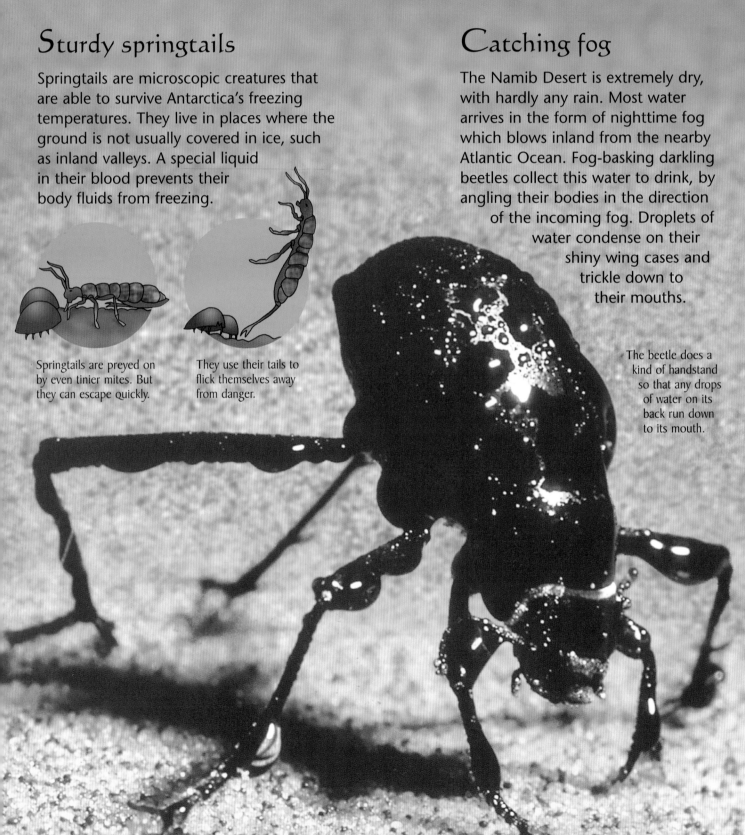

Springtails are preyed on by even tinier mites. But they can escape quickly.

They use their tails to flick themselves away from danger.

Catching fog

The Namib Desert is extremely dry, with hardly any rain. Most water arrives in the form of nighttime fog which blows inland from the nearby Atlantic Ocean. Fog-basking darkling beetles collect this water to drink, by angling their bodies in the direction of the incoming fog. Droplets of water condense on their shiny wing cases and trickle down to their mouths.

The beetle does a kind of handstand so that any drops of water on its back run down to its mouth.

Bowled over

Wheel spiders living in the dunes of the Mojave Desert use the sandy slopes to help them escape from predators. If a wheel spider feels in danger, it curls up into a ball. It can then simply roll away down the face of a sand dune, much faster than either it, or its attacker, could run.

A wheel spider can't move very fast over the slippery desert sand.

If threatened, it folds its legs underneath itself and prepares to roll away from danger.

A rolled-up wheel spider is hidden against its sandy surroundings.

INTERNET LINK
For a link to a website with lots of fascinating cockroach facts, go to
www.usborne-quicklinks.com

Rampant roaches

Cockroaches live on every continent except for Antarctica. They are so widespread because they can eat almost anything, from bat-droppings to book-bindings. They can also survive in a range of temperatures – but not below freezing. When it gets too cold, they might move into people's houses.

In warm, tropical climates, cockroaches can grow as big as the one in this photograph.

117

TAKING CONTROL

Plants can't react to their surroundings by walking, running or making noises. But they can grow in particular ways, control the amount of water they take in, or curl up and hide. Scientists can even give plants special built-in survival features using genetic engineering.

Growing up

Mushrooms are the reproductive parts of certain fungi. Spores grow in the gills – the flaps that line the underside of the mushroom's cap. As a mushroom grows, it pushes up. Once it is free of the surface it expands to open its gills. The gills hang down, so the spores fall out between them and are carried away by the wind to new homes.

Spores drop down and are blown away.

Disappearing leaves

The mimosa plant has a clever way of dealing with a grazing animal. Instead of letting itself be eaten, it quickly hides its juicy leaves by folding them away, in the hope that the animal will lose interest and leave it alone.

Mushrooms growing out of a tree trunk adjust their direction of growth so that the gills hang straight down.

Normally, a mimosa is bushy – attractive to a grazing animal like a cow.

At the slightest touch, the leaves fold up and look less appetizing.

If the cow persists, whole branches droop to reveal prickly thorns on the stem.

118

This microscopic view of part of a leaf shows two open stomata.

Hole control

Plants depend on water to survive. They need the right amount inside them to work properly. They gather water through their roots and it escapes through tiny holes, called stomata, on the underside of their leaves.

When the plant contains enough water, its cells are swollen and the stomata stay open. They let water out. If the plant doesn't have enough water, its cells become floppy. Then the stomata are closed, so no more water is lost. They also close at night.

Most stomata are found on the underside of a plant's leaves, as shown by the green dots.

Plants to order

All living things have sets of chemical instructions, called genes, in their cells. Genes give living things their characteristics. Scientists can add genes to plants to give them different characteristics. For instance, plants can be grown that are more resistant to disease or pests. Plants adapted in this way are said to be genetically engineered, or genetically modified.

These leaves are from an unhealthy potato plant. Genetic engineering can make new types of plants that are more hardy, or poisonous to pests.

INTERNET LINK
For a link to a website all about the issues surrounding GM crops, go to www.usborne-quicklinks.com

PARTY TRICKS

Sea creatures have some special ways to catch prey and shake off enemies. Sharks use electrical impulses to seek out their prey. Hagfish tie themselves in knots to get away. One cunning octopus even does impersonations of other creatures.

A mimic octopus can look like a poisonous flatfish...

...or a venomous lionfish with spines outstretched...

Adaptable octopus

The mimic octopus is a recently discovered creature, capable of looking like several other, more dangerous, creatures in order to escape predators. It does this by arranging its arms and body in different ways to change shape.

...or even a highly poisonous sea snake, by burying six of its legs.

Slimy surprise

Hagfish are long and thin, and look similar to eels. They have a secret weapon that they use to fend off predators – slime. The slime is released from glands along the sides of a hagfish's body. It is made of proteins and sugars, and is thick, stringy and elastic. It forms a protective coating around the hagfish.

If it feels threatened, a hagfish can suddenly produce an enormous amount of slime which coats its body.

The hagfish can also tie itself in a knot which it moves along its body. This is useful for cleaning off old slime.

Dropping arms

A brittlestar feeds by burying itself in sand, up to the base of its arms. It waves these in the water to catch tiny creatures, which it moves to its mouth in the middle of its body. But the waving arms also attract fish, which nibble them or try to tug the brittlestar free of the sand. It is able to let part, or all, of an arm snap off. A new arm will grow from the stump.

All the brittlestar's organs are contained within the central part of its body. This explains how it can lose arms and still survive. In this photograph, the brittlestar is perched on some red coral.

Sensitive shark

All sharks have sensitive organs that pick up the electrical signals given off by other creatures in the water. But hammerhead sharks have wide, hammer-shaped heads, which are covered in these organs for extra sensitivity. They can even detect rays buried under the sandy sea floor.

A hammerhead shark swims along the sea bed, moving its hammer from side-to-side in a sweeping motion.

It detects the ray's heartbeat from under the sand. The shark scoops the ray out of its hiding place and eats it.

A hammerhead's eyes and nostrils are on the ends of its hammer.

INTERNET LINK

For a link to a website where you can find out more about sharks' senses, go to www.usborne-quicklinks.com

Hammerhead sharks also have an especially good sense of smell, for seeking out prey. They have a nostril on each end of the hammer. This allows them to decide what direction a scent is coming from, and so track down their prey.

This is the last view an unfortunate ray might see – a hammerhead shark coming in for the kill, having detected its heartbeat.

EXTRA FEATURES

Some reptiles and amphibians use special senses or sneaky tricks to help them survive. Extra senses may allow a reptile to hunt in the dark, for instance, or taste its surroundings. Creatures have surprising ways of making a quick getaway, too.

Heat seeker

Pit vipers have special sensory organs just in front of their eyes which can detect tiny changes in temperature – as little as 0.003°C (0.005°F). A viper follows heat sources to seek out warm-blooded prey, such as rodents. This extra sense means that the snake doesn't need vision to track its prey. It can hunt at night, or even deep down in dark burrows.

The pits just in front of the viper's eyes, on either side of its face, are heat-sensing organs.

Pit

Extra eye

Tuataras are reptiles, with a body design that has stayed unchanged for millions of years. They live in New Zealand, and are capable of withstanding much lower temperatures than other reptiles – as low as 12°C (54°F). Perhaps their most amazing feature is a hidden eye, which is completely covered by skin.

A tuatara may use the third eye as a daylight sensing device, because it can probably detect sunlight. The eye has a lens, and there is even a hole in the skull in front of it, but this is completely covered by skin and scales.

Third eye is under here.

A heroic tail

Many lizards' tails break off easily, if they are attacked. It is better for a lizard to survive without a tail than to be eaten. A tail is a useful piece of lizard equipment, though – it helps it to balance – and so sometimes, a lizard will grow a replacement tail.

INTERNET LINK
For a link to a website where you can find out about some really amazing animal senses, go to www.usborne-quicklinks.com

Muscles in the tail stump contract around the wound to prevent too much bleeding.

Tasting the air

Nile monitors, like other lizards and snakes, use their tongues to taste the air. They flick their forked tongues in and out, picking up tiny scent particles from the air. These particles are rubbed over the entrances to a sensitive organ inside the lizard's mouth. This helps the lizard to identify other animals nearby – prey or perhaps a possible mate.

A Nile monitor lizard flicks its tongue in and out to sense its surroundings.

On a roll

Mount Lyell salamanders are perfectly equipped for getting around their rocky home, on the slopes of the Sierra Nevada mountains in North America. They have webbed feet which cling to the steep, rocky surfaces. They also use the tip of their tail like an extra leg to help them climb. If they feel threatened, they simply roll away down the slopes to safety.

If it is touched, the Mount Lyell salamander will curl up into a ball.

The salamander rolls and bounces down the mountain, unable to control its direction.

SIGHT AND FLIGHT

Sight is vital to most birds, to help them catch prey. Birds have huge eyes, packed with special cells to give them sharp sight. Another feature that all birds share is a coat of feathers to keep them warm, dry and help them to fly.

Non-stop sight

Birds of prey depend on their excellent vision to spot and catch prey. Most have a transparent film, or membrane, that regularly moves across the surface of each eye, to keep them clean and moist. This means that the birds don't often need to blink with their eyelids, so they don't lose vital seconds of sight during the chase.

Near the back of this hawk's eye you can just see the edge of the transparent film that keeps it clean and moist.

A hawk keeps its eyes fixed on its prey from the moment it spots it.

Enormous eyes

Compared to the size of their heads, birds' eyes are many times larger than humans'. An owl's eyes are so enormous that there is no room left in its head for muscles to move the eyes. It must move its whole head to look in a different direction. It can turn its head around by 180° to look behind itself. The eyes are also packed with cells called rod cells, which help it to see very well in dark or dim light.

An owl can see in light that is 100 times poorer than people can see in.

Fabulous feathers

The feathers that birds use to fly have a central shaft with a flat vane either side. The vanes are made of barbs which hook together. This structure is strong, light and flexible – all the features which make it possible for birds to fly. Feathers also give birds a warm and waterproof covering.

Flight feathers have a central shaft with a flat vane made of hooked barbs on either side.

Barbs

Vane

Barb

Shaft

Down feathers have barbs that don't interlock, so the feather looks fluffy. These keep birds warm.

The photograph on the right shows a magnified view of a swallow's feather, showing the hooks, called barbules, which lock the barbs together.

INTERNET LINK
For a link to a website featuring champion birds – the highest, the fastest and the oldest – go to **www.usborne-quicklinks.com**

Solar power

Roadrunners have their own built-in solar panels to make the most of the Sun's energy. During the cold desert nights, a roadrunner rests. But when the Sun rises, the bird soaks up its rays through a black patch of skin on its back. By warming itself thoroughly, it can gather enough energy to run very quickly after prey.

When a roadrunner is fully warmed up, it can reach speeds of over 24kph (15mph). It chases lizards, snakes and even hummingbirds.

SUPER SENSES

Many mammals have one, highly developed sense or special ability which helps them survive. This might be one of the five senses that we have or it could be an extra, sixth sense.

Half asleep

Dolphins live in water but breathe air. They must decide to come to the surface every time they need to take a breath. They also need to sleep for a certain amount of time every day. So that they get enough rest, and still remember to breathe, dolphins sleep with only half their brain at a time. The other half stays awake, to decide when to breathe.

Starring nose

Most moles use their sense of touch to get around underground and seek out prey. A star-nosed mole has a snout ringed by extremely touch-sensitive tentacles. These twitch constantly, helping the mole to feel its way through the darkness and find food.

A dolphin sleeps with one eye closed. The other is alert to possible danger.

It sleeps just below the surface of the water. Its bones are light so it doesn't sink.

Every few minutes, it flips its tail and rises to the surface. It opens its blowhole to let out stale air and take in fresh.

When the mole finds food, the tentacles on its snout fold back out of the way while it eats. It has huge claws to shovel soil out of its way.

Each one of a tarsier's eyes weighs more than its tiny brain. The eyes are 1.6cm (0.6in) across.

Super-size eyes

Tarsiers are small mammals that live in trees and hunt at night. They have the largest eyes, compared to their body size, of any animal. They need to be able to see their insect prey in the dark. Because the eyes are so big, they don't move in their sockets. Like owls, tarsiers can turn their heads around to see behind them.

A tarsier can twist its head 180° in either direction, like an owl.

INTERNET LINK
For a link to a website about nocturnal creatures, go to **www.usborne-quicklinks.com**

Freezing with fear

If it is extremely frightened, an opossum may pretend to be dead. Its act can be so convincing that a predator, such as a fox or a dog, will leave it alone. The predator seems to believe that the opossum really is dead, even when it has been moving around normally only moments before. An opossum can stay completely still for up to four hours, if necessary.

If an opossum is threatened by a predator, it may run, growl, belch or even urinate to try to scare the predator away.

If it is completely terrified, it freezes. It rolls over, lets its tongue hang out, becomes stiff and hardly breathes.

A predator may be fooled into thinking the opossum is dead. Preferring live meat, it will usually leave the opossum alone.

TINY BUT AMAZING

Insects have very small bodies but they pack in some incredible features. Silk, one of our most luxurious fabrics, is made from threads produced by moth caterpillars. Another type of insect has a drill on its body that can penetrate wood. Insects have powerful senses, too.

Male moths use their feathery antennae to pick up the scent of females.

Feathery feelers

Moths usually fly at night, using their long antennae to smell their way around. The antennae are feathery and covered in tiny hairs, to increase their surface area. This makes them extremely sensitive. As well as smell, the antennae detect movement. Moths mainly use them to find food and to follow the scent of a possible mate.

Each branch of an antenna is covered in sensitive hairs. The antennae can detect a female moth over 1.5km (1 mile) away.

INTERNET LINK
For a link to a website with fascinating facts about insects, go to www.usborne-quicklinks.com

Many eyes

Most insects have compound eyes. These are made up of thousands of single eyes. Some dragonflies have up to 30,000 eyes in their compound eyes. Each single eye provides a different image, which merges with the others to give the insect one large, fragmented view.

Compound eyes can't move or focus, but are probably able to detect movement.

Each single eye in a compound eye is called an ommatidium. It has a lens and a cone of cells behind which make an image.

Spinning silk

Silkworms make their cocoons out of long, silk threads. Over four thousand years ago, people found that these threads could be collected and woven to make silk fabric. Silk makes beautiful clothes. It is light and very strong, but also soft and luxurious.

A silkworm caterpillar begins to make a silk cocoon. It spins the silk into a long, continuous thread, using a spinneret on its lip.

The caterpillar changes into a moth inside the cocoon. The moth dissolves one end of the silk cocoon with saliva, then comes out.

Boring insects

Ichneumon wasps lay their eggs inside the bodies of wood-boring insect larvae. The wasps track down larvae by sensing the vibrations made as they chew through wood. A wasp uses a long tube to drill through the wood and into the larva to lay its eggs. Scientists think the tube may be tipped with a kind of metal that makes it hard enough to bore through wood.

The tube is stored inside a sheath.

Tube

An ichneumon wasp drills into the bark of a tree. The tube may be up to 7.5cm (3in) long.

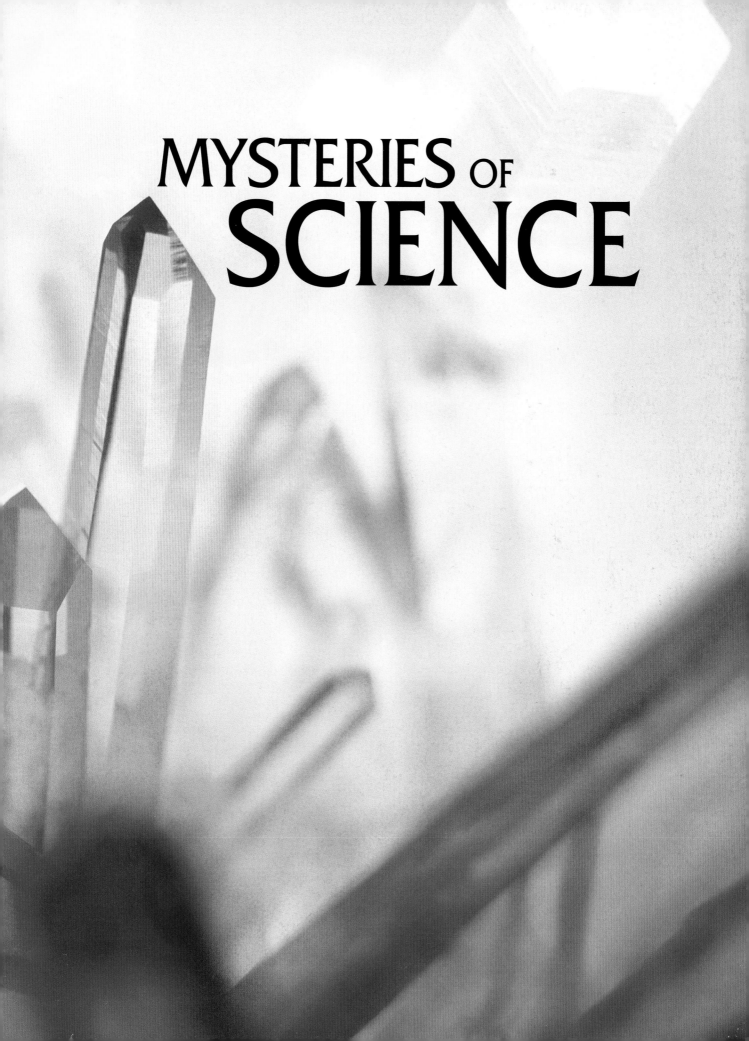

MYSTERIES OF
SCIENCE

MYSTERIOUS WORLD

Why does the Sun rise? What is fire? Where do colours come from? If you're curious about the mysteries of the world, you may have the makings of a scientist. Science begins with wonder, but goes further, using reason and imagination to look for explanations.

Scientific method

Scientists investigate all sorts of things, but they all seek knowledge in the same basic way, known as scientific method. This is a well-organized version of everyday reasoning. It involves looking at the world, guessing how part of it works, predicting what should happen if your guess is right, then testing your predictions.

You notice apples falling from a tree, and wonder if heavy things hit the ground more quickly than light things. You guess they do.

You predict that a large block of modelling clay will hit the ground before a small one.

Scientists look carefully at the world, not taking for granted what they will find. This scientist is studying a frog very closely.

You test your idea by dropping both blocks from the same height. They hit the ground together. You were wrong, so you rethink your idea, and start a new test.

All sorts

If you think that all scientists wear white coats and lurk in laboratories, then you're wrong. Scientists can be found climbing trees in the rainforest, or diving in coral reefs, discovering new animals and plants. Some are building intelligent robots, or are deep underground probing the basic particles of matter. Still others are looking back to the dawn of time, studying the birth of the universe with powerful telescopes.

Just a century ago, some scientists thought that science had few questions left to answer. Today, scientists know that they have barely begun their quest for knowledge: the world is more mysterious and marvellous than ever.

The homes of many sea plants and animals around the world are being destroyed by pollution. This scientist is testing a man-made structure that has become a new home for sea creatures.

INTERNET LINKS
Have a go at being a scientist: to find links to some experiments you can try for yourself, go to **www.usborne-quicklinks.com**

Just a theory?

People sometimes say, "Oh, that's only a theory...", meaning that it's just a guess with no proof. To scientists, a theory is just the opposite: it's a guess that has stood the test of time. For instance, in 1686, the scientist Isaac Newton published his theory of gravity, explaining how things fall and how the planets orbit the Sun.

Newton's theory was a success for hundreds of years. Yet in the 20th century, the scientist Albert Einstein published a theory that better explains how gravity works in extreme conditions. This does not overturn Newton's theory, but it shows why even the best theories are never called facts: new evidence may always be found.

THE SMALLEST SCALE

A grain of sand seems tiny, but if you could zoom inside one, you would see that it is made up of trillions of pieces, called atoms. In fact, there are probably more atoms in a grain of sand than there are grains of sand on all the beaches of the world.

Inside atoms

All things are made of atoms, yet atoms are made up of even smaller pieces called protons, neutrons and electrons. Protons have a positive electric charge; electrons have a negative charge. Neutrons have no charge so are said to be neutral.

There are various types of atom, and each type has a certain number of protons and electrons. In any one atom, the number of protons and electrons is equal. So, for each positive charge, there is a negative charge to cancel it out, leaving atoms with no overall charge. Sometimes atoms gain or lose electrons, and become charged particles called ions.

In the middle of an atom, particles called protons and neutrons are joined into a tight mass, called the nucleus, while electrons buzz around it.

Atoms in diagrams are often shown as solid balls. This diagram gives an idea of what's going on inside.

Atoms are mostly empty space, and this diagram isn't to scale. If an atom were the size of the Earth, its nucleus would be the size of a basketball, with cherry-sized electrons orbiting in the outer regions of the atmosphere.

Smaller still

Protons and neutrons are made up of even tinier particles called quarks, stuck tightly together by particles called gluons. There are six types (called flavours) of quark, known as up, down, top, bottom, strange and charm. Protons and neutrons are made of up and down quarks.

Up quark

Down quark

Gluons

Proton

Protons are made up of three smaller particles called quarks. The force that binds them together is the strongest in the universe. It is carried by particles called gluons.

134

This computer image shows iron atoms that have been nudged into a circle on a copper surface with a microscopic metal tip. The ripples show how electric charge is spread out across the copper.

Seeing atoms

Atoms are invisibly small, but they can be sensed, pictured, and even moved around, using a powerful tool called a scanning tunnelling microscope (STM). An STM has a metal tip just a few atoms wide that scans the surface of a conductor (a material electrons can move through). The tip is given a positive electrical charge and electrons on the surface are drawn to it, creating an electric current. The strength of the current increases near the material's surface, so, by measuring the current, the STM can build up a picture of the atomic landscape.

INTERNET LINK
For a link to a website where you can build a virtual carbon atom, go to
www.usborne-quicklinks.com

An STM measures changes in electric current flowing to its tip, and so senses dips and bumps in the surface it scans.

If the tip is negatively charged, electrons on atoms below are repelled by it, allowing the atoms to be pushed around.

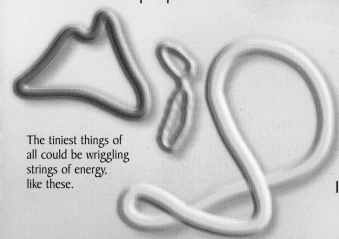

The tiniest things of all could be wriggling strings of energy, like these.

How short is a piece of string?

Some scientists think that the tiniest particles, such as quarks and electrons, are not actually little points, but are vibrations made by strings of energy, called superstrings, ten thousand billion times smaller. It can be helpful to think of quarks and electrons as being like different musical notes played on identical strings.

135

BUILDING BLOCKS

Substances with just one type of atom in them are called elements. There are 90 elements found in nature, like a set of building blocks from which everything is made. Each element's atoms have a unique number of protons and electrons, affecting the way it acts.

Gold is one of the few elements that is found in nature in its pure form. Here, it is embedded in quartz crystal, which is made up of the elements silicon and oxygen.

Weighty matters

Gold is one of the heaviest elements because its atoms hold so many protons and neutrons. The simplest and lightest element is hydrogen, because its atoms each have just one proton and one electron (and electrons weigh next to nothing).

Add another proton, neutron and electron to a gold atom and you have a mercury atom. All elements heavier than this have radioactive forms. Radioactive elements slowly lose particles from their atoms, breaking down into lighter, stable elements whose atoms won't break down further. For instance, the radioactive element uranium will, over billions of years, turn into a stable piece of lead.

INTERNET LINK
To find out more about the periodic table and play an elements game, go to www.usborne-quicklinks.com

Sticking together

Atoms are rarely found alone, and most elements are made up of clumps of atoms called molecules, or large networks of atoms called lattices. Atoms of one element can bond together with atoms of another to make a vast range of new substances, called compounds. The making or breaking-up of compounds is called a chemical reaction.

Helium is one of the few elements that exist as single atoms.

Oxygen atoms stick together in molecule pairs.

Quartz is a compound of silicon and oxygen atoms joined up in a three-dimensional lattice.

Electric connections

Many chemical reactions show signs that you can see, such as the explosion below. What you don't see is that, as the atoms rearrange and bond to form new substances, only the electrons moving across their surfaces are involved.

Electrons whizz around an atom's nucleus in a wave-like blur, but scientists find it useful to picture them grouped in shells. As atoms move closer together, electrons in one atom's outer shell are attracted to the nucleus of another. This leads to atoms bonding by giving, receiving or sharing electrons. The number of electrons in an atom's outer shell controls which atoms it will bond with. Some arrangements of electrons in shells are stable, and compounds form.

Two hydrogen atoms share electrons to form a hydrogen molecule.

Hydrogen and oxygen are explosive gases, but react to form a stable compound: water. In a water molecule, an oxygen atom gains a stable shell of eight electrons by sharing electrons with two hydrogen atoms.

Just one drop of water will start a fiery chemical reaction with a lump of potassium metal. Metal elements tend to lose electrons in reactions. Potassium atoms have just one electron to lose, so potassium reacts very easily.

Table of dreams

In 1869, a Russian chemist, Dmitri Mendeleyev, was puzzling over the 62 elements known at that time. He was trying to sort them into a table whose rows and columns of elements had things in common. One night, in a dream, he saw the answer: the table needed gaps for elements yet to be discovered. He wrote out his periodic table, as he called it, and has been proved right every time a new element has been found.

The white squares in the periodic table below show the elements discovered since Mendeleyev's day.

14	15
Si	P
Silicon	Phosphorus
32	33
Ge	As
Germanium	Arsenic

SMASHING ATOMS

If particles are given enough energy, they can whizz around at almost the speed of light. If they collide, the force can be so great that atoms smash apart, flinging out other particles as they do so. These sometimes join to form atoms of a new element.

Copying cosmic rays

Particle collisions happen in nature when cosmic rays, which are particles hurtling at high speeds through the Milky Way, crash into the Earth's atmosphere. Scientists who want to study particle collisions recreate them closer to home, using machines called particle accelerators. These machines use magnets and electricity to speed up particles into a frenzy until they crash into stationary targets or each other.

This tube creates rapidly changing electrical fields inside a particle accelerator. These changes give the particles a repetitive series of electrical "kicks" to speed them up.

Spirals like these show the paths of particles through a heated liquid in a particle detector. The liquid bubbles up where the particles pass through. A computer joins up the bubbles to show them as swirly white lines.

Crash detectives

Most particles that fly out after a particle collision travel only short distances before they start to break up. Keeping track of them is no easy task, so detecting equipment surrounds the crash sites in particle accelerators, recording the effects of each collision. The detectors produce pictures of the paths the particles have taken, helping scientists to work out the size, speed, charge and spin of these new particles.

INTERNET LINK
For a link to a website where you can watch animations and play games about the world's largest particle accelerator, go to www.usborne-quicklinks.com

Making superheavies

Scientists have created the heaviest elements ever by firing a beam of calcium atoms at a target made from americium, a metal that is most commonly used in smoke detectors. The collision created four atoms of an element that was named ununpentium.

The nucleus at the heart of each atom was crammed with 115 protons. These jostled around for space so violently that each nucleus shattered within one second, spraying out atoms of another new element. This element – which had 113 protons – was named ununtrium. Previously, the heaviest element had been Darmstadtium, with 110 protons.

This computer image shows how the world's heaviest element was created. The image shows the nucleus of a calcium atom (shown as pink) zooming towards the nucleus of an atom of americium (shown as yellow) in a particle accelerator.

Radiation zapper

Particle accelerators could be used to transform dangerous waste from nuclear power stations into harmless elements. Nuclear waste is made of unstable radioactive materials, whose atoms have so many particles moving around inside them that they give out particles. This is called high-energy radiation and can cause diseases such as cancer.

In the future, unstable radioactive materials could be zapped with beams of protons to make them split into stable elements, whose atoms contain fewer particles. These particles aren't given out but, instead, are held together inside the newly formed atoms.

Atoms of radioactive elements contain so many particles that some escape as high-energy radiation.

Bombarding radioactive atoms with proton beams changes them into atoms with fewer particles. These don't give out radiation.

CHEMICAL DETECTIVES

How can you tell one chemical from another? The way a chemical looks or smells may give you a clue to what it is. But when scientists need to identify the elements in a substance, they use their knowledge of how chemicals behave in a whole range of situations, such as when they are boiled, X-rayed or mixed with other chemicals.

Element barcodes

An element in gas form can give out coloured light rays. This happens when it is heated until it glows, and the light it produces is directed through a slit and then through a glass prism. Whereas light from the Sun can be separated into all the colours of the rainbow, the light from heated elements will only separate into rays of certain colours. Each element always produces the same set of coloured lines, like its own unique barcode.

Screen

Prism

Bar
with slit

Heated
hydrogen gas

The light from heated hydrogen gas is passed through a slit and a prism, to separate it out into rays of colour.

The X factor

Scientists can identify the structure of an element by X-raying it. When X-rays pass through an element, they hit the atoms inside it. As a result of these collisions, the X-rays change direction, and come out of the element at different angles from which they entered. The change in direction tells the scientists how the atoms inside the element are arranged. With this information, they can work out what the element is.

To produce this image, X-rays were passed through a tiny piece of gold and then recorded on electronic equipment linked to a computer. The computer turned the information into this image.

140

Ink investigation

In 1983, German scientists analysed the ink used in diaries claimed to have been written by the German Nazi leader Adolf Hitler. The tests were carried out to find out if the diaries were genuine.

Every type of black ink contains a unique mixture of dyes. Scientists scraped some ink off one of the pages, placed it onto blotting paper and dipped the end of the paper in alcohol. As the alcohol soaked upwards, it carried the ink with it. The particles in each dye travelled at different speeds up the paper, resulting in a sort of rainbow effect. This process revealed four different makes of ink in the diaries, none of which had been available when Hitler was alive: the diaries were proven to be fakes.

On each of these circular pieces of paper, a spot of ink has been separated out by a drop of alcohol, revealing the different dyes contained in the ink.

INTERNET LINK
For a link to a website where you can investigate ink online, go to
www.usborne-quicklinks.com

In the blood

Forensic scientists can detect poisons, alcohol and drugs in a sample of blood using a process called gas chromatography. The sample is heated and pushed through a coiled glass tube by a flow of helium or nitrogen gas. Each substance in the sample travels at a different speed, and any chemical that may have been dissolved in the blood is separated out. Computerized detectors at the end of the tube identify the separate substances.

Blood contains a mixture of substances. A sample is heated until it turns into a gas, which is collected in a syringe.

Nitrogen gas

The gas is injected into a glass tube. Nitrogen gas is also pumped into the tube, where it mixes with the blood.

The nitrogen gas flows through the tube, pushing the blood along and separating out its different substances.

DESIGNER MOLECULES

Until recently, it was impossible even to see atoms and molecules, but now, scientists can move them about and put them together to build things. Rearranging molecules is the key to all kinds of new medicines, materials and technology.

DNA is a chemical that can hold lots of information, so artificial molecules of it, like this one, are perfect for making tiny computers.

Body building

Despite advances in science, nature is still the master builder on an atomic scale. Scientists make many synthetic molecules by adapting ones which already exist in the natural world. For instance, DNA is a molecule found in all living things, that contains the information to create their unique features. It normally looks like a twisted ladder, but scientists have "folded" synthetic DNA into a rigid, eight-sided ball smaller than a germ. This new shape makes it much easier to build with.

Trial and error

Creating new drugs is a very important part of molecular research. Sometimes, scientists can do this by using an existing molecule's structure as a guide to making a new one. Usually, though, it's a long process of modelling many thousands of new molecules then finding out what each one does. This method is very expensive and time-consuming, but advances in computer technology have begun to make it easier.

A researcher uses goggles to view computer-generated virtual molecules, which he can also move about to see what they do.

142

Magic bullets

Researchers are trying to build molecules into "magic bullets" – drugs that target only the affected areas of the body. They hope that one day, this might allow them to treat cancer without the severe side effects caused by many anti-cancer drugs. The answer may lie in prodrugs, molecules designed to exist harmlessly in the body until they reach a tumour.

Before patients are given a prodrug, they are injected with a type of chemical called an enzyme, which attaches itself to the tumour cells.

The prodrug is like a molecular bomb which contains cell-destroying poisons. It can't go off until it makes contact with the enzyme.

The prodrug releases its poisonous contents directly into the tumour cells, which it then starts to kill. It does no harm to the rest of the body.

INTERNET LINK
For a link to a website where you can find out more about the many stages of creating a new drug, go to www.usborne-quicklinks.com

Tiny builders

In the future, molecules will be put together to make amazingly small objects, from household items to computers the size of a sugarlump. The question is, how can items that have to be built so precisely ever be mass-produced? Experts think the answer lies in microscopic robots called nanoassemblers. These incredibly small machines will use atoms not only to assemble objects, but also to make new copies of themselves. Production lines of billions of nanoassemblers could even be sent to other planets to construct space stations on their surface.

This computer image shows a miniature robot assembler grabbing bacteria in its claws. It will use these as raw materials to build more robots like itself.

143

MATTER ON THE MOVE

Everything around us is made of matter, but why are some things solid as a rock, while others flow like maple syrup or vanish like a puff of steam?

Sluggish solids

Most of the matter you see around you is solid: the house you live in, the chairs you sit on, the books you read – even the tiny specks of dust floating in the air. But what makes matter solid?

All matter is made up of tiny, moving particles called atoms, or clumps of atoms called molecules, which are drawn to each other by electrical forces. Molecules in solids don't have much energy, so, while they may joggle slightly, they stay in the same place – a bit like somebody running on the spot. This means that solid matter stays in the same shape.

This splashing water drop shows that, although liquids have no fixed shape, they take on many shapes as they move.

Go with the flow

When a solid is heated to a certain level, its molecules gain enough energy to move around more freely. The solid matter then melts into a liquid: its molecules flow easily around each other, and it loses its fixed shape. A liquid's molecules are still drawn to each other, though, so they stay together, the liquid filling a fixed amount of space. Liquids take the shape of any container they are in.

The molecules in solid objects have little energy, so they stay in the same place.

Inside a body of liquid, the molecules have enough energy to move around each other.

INTERNET LINK
For a link to a website where you can find out more about atoms, molecules and the states of matter, go to **www.usborne-quicklinks.com**

It's a gas

When liquids are heated enough, their molecules gain the energy to overcome the electrical forces that keep them together. The liquid then boils: its molecules fly free from its surface and it becomes a gas. Gases spread out to fill any space they are in. Unless they are kept in a tightly sealed container they will escape.

The energetic molecules in gases move freely, and spread out to fill any space they are in.

Breaking free

The positively charged nucleus in the middle of an atom has negatively charged electrons whizzing around it. The electrical force that attracts opposite charges stops the electrons flying off, and also joins atoms into molecules. If a gas becomes extremely hot, the atoms in its molecules gain enough energy to overcome the pull of the electrical force, and split apart from each other. Then the electrons become energetic enough to break free from the atoms. A cloud of electrons, and atoms that have lost them (ions), is formed. This is called a plasma.

In plasmas, electrons escape from their atoms. As this happens, the atoms become charged, and are called ions.

The huge amounts of energy needed to turn gas into plasma are not commonly found on Earth, but plasma does form briefly in flashes of lightning. There is a little plasma in fire, and inside fluorescent tubes, but most is found out in space. Stars, such as the Sun, are huge balls of plasma, and space itself is strewn with shining plasma clouds called bright nebulas. In fact, of the four states of matter, solids, liquids and gases make up only 1% of matter in the universe: all the rest is plasma.

These glowing streamers are plasma being created inside a glass sphere. Atoms of neon gas are being heated and ripped apart by a huge build-up of electrical charge, giving off energy in the form of pink light.

CRYSTALS

Most pure solid substances, from grains of salt to the most precious gemstones, are made up of flat-faced, straight-sided shapes called crystals.

Salt crystals are cube-shaped because the tiny particles that make them up are arranged in repeating, cube-shaped patterns.

Little goes large

The shape of crystals can vary from one substance to another. This is because the particles inside them are built up in different ways. The atoms, ions or molecules in crystals are ordered in repeating patterns called lattices, which are echoed from this tiny scale all the way up to the full-size crystal.

Sodium ion   Chloride ion

A typical grain of salt contains 100,000 billion ions arranged in a cubic lattice, like the one shown here.

Crystal crowns

Crystals appear in all sorts of natural substances, even in living things, such as microscopic viruses. Viruses are simple life-forms that live inside the cells of animals and plants. Their heads are made of a single crystal, often a 20-sided shape called an icosahedron.

These three viruses are on the surface of a much larger cell, which will help them to reproduce. The crystal shape of their heads is clear to see.

INTERNET LINK
For a link to a website where you can play some liquid crystal games, go to www.usborne-quicklinks.com

Liquid crystals,
like these ones, are
normally transparent, but the
type of light used in a polarizing
microscope makes them appear
coloured, so they are easier to see.

Liquid crystals

Liquid crystals are remarkable substances that behave like both solid crystals and liquids. In solid crystals, the particles line up in all dimensions, across the crystal's length, width and height. In liquid crystals, the particles only line up in one dimension: in other dimensions the particles can move freely, as they would in a liquid.

In a solid crystal, the molecules are lined up and locked rigidly in a fixed position.

In a liquid, the position of molecules isn't fixed, so they are able to move around freely.

In a liquid crystal, the molecules are able to move around, but only in a single direction.

When light shines through liquid crystals, it follows the direction of their molecules. If an electric current is passed through the crystals, the molecules twist around, blocking the light. This effect is used to create images on liquid crystal displays (LCDs), as on digital watches or flat computer screens.

Crystals in space

The way crystals form is affected by the force of gravity pressing down on them. In low gravity, crystals grow bigger, better and more quickly than on Earth. Scientists are using the low gravity conditions in the Space Shuttle to grow crystals of proteins – complex molecules central to the growth of living things. Studying space-grown crystals of the protein insulin, for example, may help to develop better treatments for the condition diabetes.

These insulin crystals
were grown on Earth.

These bigger ones
were grown in space.

MIXING IT UP

From the air you breathe to many of the foods you eat, nearly all the substances around you are mixtures of elements and compounds jumbled together without being chemically linked.

Millions of mixtures

The number of possible mixtures of elements and compounds is uncountable. Some mixtures have parts that can be seen by the naked eye, for example, a jar of assorted sweets. Others, like wet sand, have tinier ingredients: sand grains and microscopic water molecules. Many other mixtures contain just atoms and molecules. The air around you, for example, is an invisible mixture of gases.

As mixtures are not chemically bound, they can be separated fairly easily. Sweets are easily sorted. Wet sand can be dried out and its water collected. Even air can be separated by cooling it in a laboratory and collecting its gases as they turn to liquid at very low, but different, temperatures.

Air is a mixture of gases; mainly the elements nitrogen, oxygen and argon. (In reality, the particles would be much more spaced out than shown here.)

● Nitrogen ● Oxygen ● Argon

Vanishing act

When sugar is stirred into water, it seems to melt away and vanish. But sugar doesn't melt until it is much hotter than boiling water, so where does it go? The sugar has not melted, but dissolved: its individual molecules have spread throughout the water to make a mixture called a sugar solution. Solutions are the most finely blended of mixtures, and are always see-through, although some, such as mouthwash, have a coloured tint.

As this sugar lump dissolves, the sugar disappears into a syrupy flow which slowly spreads through the water.

INTERNET LINK
To find a website that tells you how
to make some weird slime mixtures
that are both solid and liquid, go to
www.usborne-quicklinks.com

Polystyrene foam is 95% air,
mixed with just 5% polystyrene. This
microscope image shows clumps of
air-filled polystyrene bubbles (yellow)
separated by air-filled gaps (black).

Kept in suspense

Some substances won't
mix as thoroughly as
sugar and water; others hardly
mix at all. In salad dressing, for
instance, oil floats on vinegar. When
you shake salad dressing before using
it, tiny blobs of oil are suspended in the
vinegar, turning it into a cloudy liquid
called an emulsion. Milk and mayonnaise
are other examples of emulsions.

Mixtures may also contain substances in
different states. Bread and polystyrene are
solids containing trapped gas bubbles.
Smoke is a gas carrying soot particles.

Milk contains
droplets of fat
hanging in water.

Bread is a solid
containing
bubbles of air.

Smoke is made up
of pieces of soot
floating in gas.

Liquid lenses

Scientists have used two liquids that don't easily mix
to invent a camera lens that changes shape, like the
lens in the human eye. The lens is made up of an
oil and a solution in a little plastic cylinder.

This little camera lens uses
non-mixing liquids to mimic
the lens in the human eye.

When the sides of the cylinder are
charged with an electric current,
the solution shrinks into a dome
shape at one end. The surface
where the oil and the solution
meet acts as a lens. As the
current changes, the lens
changes shape, letting it
focus at different distances.

STRANGE MATTER

INTERNET LINKS
For links to websites about dark matter and antimatter, go to
www.usborne-quicklinks.com

Nature is never as simple as you might like. Scientists are starting to discover that everyday matter, made of atoms, ions and molecules, is just a small part of the stuff that makes up the universe.

Scientists make antimatter by blasting atoms with gamma rays. This image shows the spiralling path (green) of an electron in a particle detector, as it spins off in the opposite direction to its positron antiparticle (red). The long, green track belongs to another electron.

Mirror matter

You may have heard of strange stuff called antimatter in science fiction movies – but it is science fact. Every type of matter particle has a mirror image, or antiparticle. For instance, the electron's antiparticle is the positron. It has the same mass but opposite features, such as charge.

If a particle hits its antiparticle, they are both destroyed in a burst of energy. Particles and antiparticles are created and destroyed all the time in cosmic rays, which bombard Earth from space. Scientists can make microscopic amounts of antimatter in the laboratory. They hope to make enough to power spacecraft: just a teaspoonful could send a rocket to Mars.

Mind maps

Antimatter can be used to watch people think. In PET (positron emission tomography) brain scans, radioactive sugar called FDG is injected into the brain. The brain uses energy from sugar to work, so the parts that are thinking use up the most sugar. The FDG releases antimatter positrons from these active parts of the brain. These meet their electron opposites in the brain and are destroyed, turning into waves of energy called gamma rays. These rays are detected to build up a computer map of the brain.

PET scans use antimatter to create a computer map of the brain. The red and yellow patches on this scan show parts of the brain involved in listening to music.

Missing matter mystery

In 1933, a Swiss astronomer named Fritz Zwicky was watching a group of galaxies called the Coma cluster. They were spinning so quickly that they should have flown apart. Zwicky reasoned that, just as the Sun's invisible gravity stops the Earth from flying away, there must be a large amount of stuff that can't be detected – dark matter – holding the galaxies together. Zwicky's ideas were thought far-fetched at the time, but now scientists believe that 90% of the universe may be made of this mysterious dark matter.

This X-ray satellite picture shows a cloud of hot pink gas surrounding large, white blobs, which are galaxies. Scientists think that invisible "dark matter" is holding the cloud together.

The burst of yellow rays in the image below shows a neutrino being detected. Scientists hope to weigh neutrinos accurately, as they may make up part of the universe's mass that scientists have yet to account for.

Just passing through

Not all strange forms of matter are found only in space. Did you know that every second, billions of tiny particles called neutrinos are zipping through your body, then passing through the Earth itself?

Unlike most matter particles, neutrinos are so light they seem unaffected by gravity, and have no charge, so they ignore electrical forces. It's amazing, then, that they were ever discovered by scientists. Deep in a nickel mine, in Sudbury, Canada, a plastic sphere the size of a ten-storey building, filled with heavy water (water with extra neutrons), is used to detect neutrinos. The sphere has 10,000 radiation detectors which pick up faint flashes of light from just ten neutrinos per day.

WONDERFUL WATER

Water is so widespread it's often taken for granted. Two-thirds of your body is made of water, indeed, two-thirds of the Earth is covered in it. But water is, in fact, a fascinating liquid, and the weird ways it acts make it not just useful but vital.

Stuff of life

People often think of solids as denser or heavier than liquids, but water is different. As it freezes it expands, growing less dense. That's why ice floats. Imagine what would happen in a fishpond in winter if ice were denser than liquid water: it would freeze from the bottom up – along with the fish. As it is, pond ice traps heat, so the fish survive. This is just one way in which water is vital to living things.

Oxygen   Hydrogen

Water molecules are made up of two hydrogen atoms joined to an oxygen atom, so scientists also call water H_2O (2 × Hydrogen) + (Oxygen).

As water freezes, its molecules lose heat energy and lock into an ordered hexagonal crystal pattern. There is lots of space in between, so ice is less dense than water.

Snow business

There are millions of snowflake patterns, so many that you may have even heard it said that each snowflake is different. But in one way they are nearly all the same: most snowflakes have six identical sections. This is because snowflakes grow outwards, in six directions, from a tiny hexagon of ice that has formed around a speck of dust.

The individual shapes of these snowflakes come from the changing speeds at which they grew inside snow clouds.

Liquid skin

Look at a water drop and you'll see it is shaped like a dome, as if it were held together by a transparent skin. Inside the drop, water molecules are drawn together by electrical forces like little magnets. The molecules at the surface are far more attracted to each other than to air molecules around them. This means the surface molecules hold tightly together, making the water's surface act like a stretchy skin.

This surface tension tries to pull water into the smallest shape it can: a sphere. On bodies of water larger than a drop, the force of gravity squashes the sphere flat.

Molecules at the surface of water attract each other, making a 'skin'.

INTERNET LINK
For a link to a website where you can see amazing snowflakes, go to www.usborne-quicklinks.com

This raft spider can walk on water, held up by a liquid skin. See how the skin bends under the spider's weight.

Just add water

From powder paint to instant soup, water can dissolve more substances than any other. This is because water molecules have ends with positive and negative charges, a little like magnets. Many substances contain charged particles (ions) that are attracted to these charges. This tears the substances apart. Water's dissolving powers are vital for living things. For example, water in blood carries dissolved sugar to organs that need energy.

Salt is made up of sodium and chloride ions. The charges on water molecules tug at them, pulling the salt crystal apart.

The water molecules keep pulling the sodium and chloride ions away until they are all surrounded. The salt is now dissolved in the water.

153

METAL MARVELS

Metal is one of the most useful and widely found types of material on Earth. The chances are that, no matter where you are, there's something made of metal nearby. There's even metal in your own body.

These shiny blobs are drops of mercury, the only metal that's a liquid at room temperature.

INTERNET LINK
For a link to a website where you can take part in an animated quiz to discover some amazing uses of metals, go to www.usborne-quicklinks.com

What can metals do?

Almost all metals have features that make them useful to us: electricity can flow easily through all of them, and many can be moulded, bent, beaten into sheets or stretched into wire. A few, such as iron, can be magnetized. When tiny iron particles are added to water or oil they make MR (magneto-rheological) fluid, which turns from a liquid to a solid if exposed to a magnetic field. It's very useful for strengthening buildings and bridges, as explained below.

Fluid particles

Solid particles

The support cables of this bridge in China have MR fluid shock absorbers between them. Tiny iron particles float in this fluid.

If sensors in the bridge detect vibrations from wind or earthquakes, powerful magnets around the floating particles switch on and off.

When the magnets are on, the fluid turns solid. It can switch instantly between the two states, allowing the cables to absorb any vibrations.

Memory metals

Scientists have found ways to give some metals even more useful features. Memory metals, for instance, return to their original shape after they have been twisted, hammered or pulled. They are useful in surgery because they can be bent and placed into awkward-to-reach parts of the body. When body heat warms the metal up, it returns to its correct shape.

Tooth braces made of bent memory metal change shape very slowly, gently moving the teeth as they do so.

154

All puffed up

We think of metal as mainly being heavy and solid, but it can be melted into a liquid, then blown into foam by adding bubbles of gas. When it cools and solidifies, pockets of air are trapped inside, making it like a sponge.

Metal foam has a spongy texture like normal foam, but it's much tougher. It is heat-resistant, strong, and excellent at absorbing impacts, such as in car crashes.

Metallic meals

Metal is so important, we literally couldn't survive without it. All plants and animals have minute traces of metals in them, which they need to stay alive. For example, around 2% of a person's entire body weight is a metal called calcium, almost all of which is in the teeth and bones. Plants take in metals from soil and water, and we absorb these metals when we eat plants, or animals that ate plants.

Ores and more

Most metals can be extracted from the ground, where they exist combined with other elements, as ores. These are mined, then broken down by chemicals or exposed to electricity or fierce heat to release the metals within them. A few metals, such as gold, can exist on their own because they're so unreactive, but they're more rare than normal metals.

This ancient Egyptian mask has kept its shine for thousands of years. Gold doesn't react with air and become duller the way iron and silver do.

FANTASTIC PLASTICS

Since their invention in the 19th century, plastics have revolutionized the way we live. They can be stretched, moulded, melted or woven into strands to make thousands of useful things.

What are plastics?

Plastics are polymer materials, which are made of many molecules joined up in chains. Depending on the structure of their chains, polymers can be stiff, stretchy, hard, soft or resistant to heat. That's why they're so versatile.

All-purpose plastics

It's no wonder that so many things are made of plastics – compared to other materials, such as metals, they are very cheap and easy to produce. Plastics make safe casing for wires and electrical gadgets, because electricity can't travel easily through them. They're so unreactive, some kinds can be placed inside the human body with no harmful effects. They can even be spun into fibres to make lightweight bulletproof clothing.

These are highly magnified strands of nylon, a plastic fibre, in a stocking. Nylon fibres are strong and stretchy, so they're good for making clothes.

When a bullet strikes a bulletproof vest, the many layers of woven plastic fibres inside the vest absorb the energy of the impact, protecting the wearer from harm.

Plastic farming

Since plastics are so widely used, researchers are always looking for new ways of mass-producing them. Amazingly, in the future, plastic might be grown as a crop, using bacteria that can create it naturally. When scientists add genes (chemical instructions) from these bacteria to a type of plant called thale cress, plastic grows in the plant's green cells. One day, fields full of "plastic plants" might be a common sight.

This image shows tiny orange blobs of plastic growing inside the cells of a cress plant. The cells are shown at 10,000 times their real size.

Teaming up

Although plastics are useful on their own, they can be combined with materials such as carbon, metal or glass to make even better materials called composites. One of the most ingenious features of plastic composites is that they have the strength of the materials they are combined with, but weigh much less. This means they're ideal for making aircraft parts, the outer shells of racing cars and other things which need to be light, but incredibly tough.

INTERNET LINK
For a link to a website where you can make your own plastics in an interactive lab, go to www.usborne-quicklinks.com

Coming apart

Millions of plastic items are thrown out worldwide every year, and that adds up to a lot of rubbish. For many years, plastics have been made using petrochemicals, which come from oil. Most plastic of this kind takes several hundred years to biodegrade, or break down naturally. But scientists are now developing a type of plastic made from cornstarch, which biodegrades much more quickly.

Water
Soil
Plastic
Cornstarch

Biodegradable plastic is buried in a dump. The cornstarch absorbs water from the soil and expands.

When it's full of water, the cornstarch erupts. The force breaks the plastic around it into little pieces.

Bacteria

Bacteria in the soil can break down the tiny bits of plastic more quickly than one big piece.

COOL CARBON

Carbon is a real wonder element. It is found throughout the universe in suns, in planets' atmospheres, and in living things. An average person contains 16kg (35lb) of carbon combined with other elements.

Kinds of carbon

Pure carbon has three very different basic forms: graphite, diamond and fullerenes, such as Buckminsterfullerine (also called buckyballs). Soft, flaky graphite is probably best known as the "lead" in a pencil. Diamond, on the other hand, is the hardest substance in nature. A diamond-tipped drill can cut through granite as easily as a saw cuts through wood.

In graphite, the atoms link up like layers of chicken wire. The layers move smoothly over each other, making graphite a good lubricant. Electricity can also flow through it easily.

A diamond's atoms are more closely packed together than in any other substance. This is what gives diamonds their incredible hardness.

The atoms in buckyballs form a hollow ball. Their unusual structure makes them immensely strong – a hundred times stronger than steel, but only one-sixth of its weight.

Diamond is a type of carbon which takes millions of years to form. This diamond has been cut and polished to make it sparkle.

The molecule of life

Life as we know it couldn't exist without carbon. The chemicals that make up living things are incredibly complex, and only carbon can form bonds with other atoms in enough combinations to create them. So if life exists elsewhere in the universe, it is probably carbon-based too – in fact, some scientists think that the carbon that everyone is made of was created in the hearts of distant stars.

Tiny technology

Nanotechnology is the science of extremely small things. Nanomaterials, which are less than ten-thousandths of a millimetre in size, can be used to build on a tinier scale than ever before. Microscopic graphite cylinders called nanotubes are a type of nanomaterial that will be widely used in the future. They can be added to other materials to give them unbeatable strength, or used to make electronic devices 100 times smaller than today's.

These colourful spikes show the electrical field created by the peapod's carbon atoms.

The image on the right is a computer model of a "peapod", a nanotube that's been filled with buckyballs to increase its strength.

INTERNET LINK
For a link to a website where you can see what new materials you can make from virtual carbon, go to **www.usborne-quicklinks.com**

Carbon dating

Carbon-14 is a radioactive form of carbon found in the air and in natural objects, such as wood and bones. Like all radioactive materials, it breaks down into smaller amounts over time. Every 5,700 or so years, there is half as much carbon-14 in an object as there was before. Scientists can learn how old something is by comparing the amount of carbon-14 left in it with the amount that was originally there, a technique known as carbon dating.

This is the mummified body of a man. By measuring the amount of radioactive carbon-14 it contains, scientists have worked out that he lived around 2,000 years ago.

STUNNING SILICON

Silicon is the second most common element on Earth. Combined with other elements, it makes all kinds of materials that can be used for building, storing data or travelling into space. Silicon is most commonly used in making glass.

This highly magnified image shows a microscopic creature called a diatom. Its body is protected by a hard, glassy case made of silica, with intricate patterns on its surface.

Nature's glass

We normally think of glass as an artificial material, but nature made it first. In fact, some living things, such as the water creature in the picture above, have a natural glass called silica in their bodies. Silica, a combination of silicon and oxygen, is also the main ingredient of obsidian, a glassy rock formed in the searing heat of volcanoes.

Shiny black obsidian stones like this one were originally liquid rock, which flowed out of an erupting volcano and cooled rapidly.

Man-made glass

For at least 9,000 years, people have been using sand, a mineral containing silica, to make glass. It was originally just a decorative material, but today glass has many more uses, enabling people to light their homes, transmit information and see well. The feature of glass that makes it so suitable for all these jobs is its transparency. In fact, the type of glass inside fibre-optic cables, very fine glass tubes which are used for communication, is pure and clear enough to make a window several kilometres thick that would still be perfectly see-through.

Chips with that?

Extremely thin slices of silicon are etched with millions of microscopic components, called transistors, to make computer microchips. As technology advances, computers need more and more transistors on each microchip to hold information. Eventually, etching won't be able to produce transistors which are small enough, so scientists have found a way to imprint more intricate chips than ever before using a laser.

Mould

To make a computer chip, a silicon slice is placed next to a tiny quartz mould shaped like many transistors, with features as tiny as one hundred thousandth of the width of a human hair.

Laser pulse   Silicon slice

A laser pulse is shone through the quartz for 20 billionths of a second, melting the top layer of silicon.

Melted silicon

When it cools, the silicon is left imprinted with the mould's shape.

Silicate ceramics

Many years ago, people found that baking silicate minerals such as clay and feldspar turned them into hard ceramics that did not wear out with age. These were traditionally used to make bricks and tableware but today, ceramics have more hi-tech uses too, from super-sharp knives to engine parts and rocket nose cones. The Space Shuttle is protected from temperatures of up to 1,600°C (2,912°F) by a layer of ceramic tiles.

INTERNET LINK
For a link to a website where you can find fun facts and videos about glass, aerogel and silicon crystals, go to **www.usborne-quicklinks.com**

Hit and mist

Aerogel is an ultra-light man-made material. It contains silica, but most of it – 99.8% – is air, which makes it look like a transparent mist. Despite its ghostly appearance, it's both solid to the touch and very heat-resistant. When tiny objects hit aerogel, they become embedded in it, so NASA scientists use it to collect debris from the tails of comets to bring back to Earth and study.

Aerogel looks very delicate, but it is strong enough to support this glass dish and pile of matches, protecting them from the hot, blue flame of burning gas.

NATURE'S IDEAS

For hundreds of years, people have been trying to create materials that meet the demands of their basic needs and changing lifestyles. Although many of these materials are created in a lab, the inspiration is often provided by nature.

Nature knows best

All living creatures, including humans, face challenges. Animals and plants cope with difficulties in surprisingly ingenious ways, sometimes using natural materials that amaze and baffle scientists. For instance, mussels stick themselves to rocks using a natural, waterproof glue in their bodies that's stronger than any man-made glue in existence.

The shell on the right is lined with mother-of-pearl, a natural ceramic. This contains a mix of chemicals that gives it 3,000 times more strength than the chalk that the shell is mostly made of. Scientists still don't know how that's possible.

INTERNET LINKS
For links to websites where you can study many different materials and find out what it takes to be a materials scientist, go to www.usborne-quicklinks.com

Finding the answer

Scientists often make discoveries by asking, "How do other living things deal with this problem, and how can we copy them?" Using science to imitate nature is called biomimicry, and it often finds solutions in the most unlikely places. Imagine, for example, that you wanted to develop a material that's waterproof and self-cleaning. Scientists have found that lotus leaves possess both of these properties, so they set about unlocking the secret of how they work.

When rainwater falls on a lotus plant leaf, the water forms a ball and rolls off, taking dirt with it. The leaf stays dry and clean – but how?

The answer lies in the leaf's highly waterproof waxy coating. Scientists learned its recipe, and are mass-producing a synthetic version.

Gecko glue

Geckos are a type of lizard with the ability to cling to surfaces at any angle, even upside-down. They do this using electrically charged hairs on the soles of their feet, which are attracted to anything they touch. A material with such strong stickiness would be useful to humans, so scientists have created "gecko tape" – a strip of plastic covered in millions of synthetic hairs, like a gecko's foot – and on a smaller scale, nano-velcro.

This image shows the pads made of millions of tiny hairs which give a gecko's feet their super sticking power.

Nano-velcro, made of tiny hooked carbon tubes (nanotubes), mimics the gecko's hairs. It is 30 times more powerful than normal glue.

Super silk

Spider silk is one of nature's most marvellous materials – a lightweight fibre that's five times stronger, weight for weight, than steel. Scientists are keen to use these properties in synthetic materials, but the silk is hard to make in bulk. So far, they have found a way to mass-produce silk-making chemicals in the milk of some goats, by changing the goats' body chemistry.

These mushroom-shaped mounds are spinnerets, the parts of a spider's body which silk comes from. Fresh silk (shown here in blue) is oozing out.

INVESTIGATING ENERGY

What's everywhere, but can't be seen? What do you use all the time, but hardly ever notice? The answer is energy – the thing that is needed to make every action in the universe happen.

INTERNET LINK
For a link to a website where you can help a mad scientist create a monster by saving energy, go to www.usborne-quicklinks.com

What can energy do?

Energy can do literally everything. Machines need it to function, living things need it to live, and no movement can take place without it. Different kinds of energy include light, sound and heat.

When you strike a match, it makes heat and light energy. Before the match was struck, though, that energy was stored in the chemicals on its head.

Eternal energy

If energy is everywhere, making things happen, where does it come from, and what happens if it runs out? Actually, all the energy that exists now was created at the same time as the universe itself. It never gets used up, just moved around – for instance, when coal is burned in power stations to make electrical energy. But this energy isn't new: it already existed inside the coal.

Millions of years ago, the Earth was covered with plants. They grew using energy from the Sun.

The plants died with the energy stored inside them. Over time, their remains were crushed under the ground and became coal.

Today, coal is burned to release the energy that was trapped inside the plants all those years ago.

All change

Energy can never be created or destroyed, only changed from one form to another. This is called the Law of Conservation of Energy. Whenever any action takes place, energy is being changed.

Hold a pencil in the air. Chemical energy from food in your body turns into kinetic (movement) energy as you raise your arm.

The pencil now has potential energy, because it has been lifted against the force of gravity: if you drop it, it will fall.

As it drops, the pencil has kinetic energy. When it hits the ground, this becomes sound energy, and you hear a noise.

Energy unleashed

An enormous amount of energy is stored in the heart of every atom. It's called nuclear energy, because it is released when the nucleus of an atom is split apart. Unlike other reactions, where one type of energy is converted to another, nuclear reactions make energy from matter. This is possible because matter is like stored energy, in that it too cannot be created or destroyed.

The physicist Albert Einstein worked out that a very small amount of mass, another word for matter, can be made into a vast amount of energy. That's how nuclear power works – atoms of a nuclear fuel, such as uranium, are split inside a reactor to release the stores of energy inside them.

This pool-type nuclear reactor, used for research and training, produces much less energy than a power plant.

The pool water keeps the reactor core stable.

POWER TO THE PEOPLE

Over the years, people have come to depend on more and more energy to provide heat, light, electricity and transport. Most of this energy comes from burning fossil fuels such as gas, oil and coal. But these won't last forever.

INTERNET LINK
For a link to a website where you can play games about power, go to www.usborne-quicklinks.com

Fuels of the future

Experts think that before this century ends, there will be no oil or gas left. The race is on to find the best alternatives for a fossil fuel-free future. Renewable energy sources like the ones on this page are a good option, as they won't ever run out. But most of them are limited as to where or how they can be used. Scientists are constantly looking for cheaper, cleaner and more convenient sources of renewable energy.

This is a wind farm in California. A device called a turbine changes movement energy from these giant blades into electrical energy. Wind power is one of many alternatives to fossil fuel.

Cleaner cars

People's power needs aren't limited to electricity for homes and workplaces. Cars and other vehicles use fossil fuels too, releasing damaging gases into the atmosphere as they go. Ideally, vehicles of the future need to run on a clean, plentiful power source that doesn't hurt the environment. With this in mind, scientists have developed hydrogen fuel cells. Hydrogen gas is freely available, and creates no harmful exhaust fumes.

Hydrogen

Oxygen

Water molecules

Inside a fuel cell, hydrogen and oxygen atoms join together and release energy. The only by-product of this chemical reaction is H_2O – ordinary water.

Natural energy

Living things gain the energy that they use to grow from the Sun, which makes them miniature powerhouses – as long as you can find a way to use them. Landfills, farming and some kinds of industrial processes, such as paper-making, all produce large amounts of energy-filled natural matter. Also known as biomass, this mostly consists of dung, dead plants and wood pulp. To release its energy it can be burned as it is, or processed into chemical fuels such as ethanol.

Biomass energy can come from any natural source – including animals' bodies. In some countries, animal dung is widely used as a fuel.

Cow dung is gathered, mixed with straw and left to dry. These dung pancakes can then be burned to heat homes or make cooking fires.

Plasma power

Today's nuclear power plants produce energy by breaking down atoms, but one day they may use nuclear fusion – that is, joining atoms together. Fusion releases huge amounts of energy in the form of unimaginably hot plasma. In theory, fusion plasma could provide the whole world with plentiful renewable energy, but scientists don't yet know how to control its awesome power.

Nuclear fusion in the Sun's core is what keeps it burning. Here, loops of searing hot plasma are flaring from its surface.

FEELING THE FORCE

Forces are pushing and pulling around you all the time, although you might not always realize they're there. Right now, forces are helping to hold your body together and keeping it on the ground.

Forces at large

Forces are ways in which things affect each other. Sometimes you can see what forces do, like the force of a bat hitting a ball, but some work on levels only scientists can observe. Physical forces, the type that can be seen in the world around you, work in pairs. For instance, if something pushes forwards, there must be a force pushing backwards too. When you're standing on the ground, the Earth is actually pushing up with the same force.

Rockets are powered by pairs of forces. Jets of super-powerful exhaust gas shoot backwards out of the rocket, propelling it upwards at the same time.

Keep on moving

Objects tend to resist changes in movement. This means that you need a force to start something moving, and it then continues to move unless another force affects it. In theory, this tendency, called inertia, should keep a moving object going forever, but everyone knows that perpetual motion like this doesn't happen. That's because of a force called friction, which is created when surfaces rub together. For centuries, inventors tried to build perpetual motion machines, but friction makes it impossible on Earth.

Dolphins have smooth, sleek bodies to overcome friction in water.

Objects in space can keep moving because there's no air, so no friction.

168

The fantastic four

Forces also exist on much tinier and more immense scales than the pushes and pulls between everyday objects. Physicists think there are four fundamental forces which define how matter, and the universe itself, is held together.

Gravitational force keeps the Earth in orbit around the Sun.

Gravitational force is an attraction between two objects. It's very weak – a trillion trillion times weaker than the strong nuclear force – but has an infinite range.

Atom

Electron

Nucleus

Neutron

Neutron

Proton

The electromagnetic or EM force controls the way that any particle with an electrical charge behaves. It's also responsible for magnetism and light waves, and holds together the electrons and nucleus of an atom.

The weak nuclear force allows particles inside atoms to break down over time. This diagram shows a neutron breaking down into three smaller particles.

The strong nuclear force is the strongest force in nature, but it only works on an atomic scale. It tightly binds together the protons and neutrons in an atom's nucleus.

Life without forces

The fundamental forces are so important, a universe without them would be hard to imagine. For a start, matter couldn't exist. Protons naturally repel each other, so without the strong nuclear force to hold them together, the nucleus of every atom would blow apart like a nuclear bomb. The EM force is also essential, keeping every atom's electrons in place – otherwise the universe would be an infinite soup of random particles.

INTERNET LINK
For a link to a website where you can play a game demonstrating the power of the four forces, go to www.usborne-quicklinks.com

The weak nuclear force allows radioactive decay and nuclear fusion to take place. Since the Sun is fuelled by this process, without the weak force it would stop burning. Darkness would cover the Earth, and life as we know it would fizzle out.

GRIPPING GRAVITY

If you jump up into the air, just a little or as high as you can, you'll always fall back to the ground. Your body is pulled towards the Earth by a mysterious force called gravity.

Pulling together

Gravity is a force that attracts things to each other. The bigger something is, the stronger its gravitational force. Earth is massive, so its gravity is strong enough to attract everything on its surface towards it. But even small things, like your hand and this book, have a force of gravity attracting them together. It's just too weak to feel.

The smaller the object, the weaker its gravity. The Moon is one-sixth the size of the Earth, so astronauts leap around easily in its weak gravity.

A planet larger than Earth would have stronger gravity. An astronaut on its surface would find it hard to stand, never mind leap.

Weight watching

Everything that's made of something has mass, and everything that has mass also has a weight when it's being affected by gravity. The weight depends on the mass of the objects involved, and the distance between their centres of gravity. Earth's centre of gravity is literally in its centre, and yours is roughly around your navel. The further apart these two things are, the less you weigh, although the change is very slight.

Black holes

A black hole is the remains of a star that has collapsed in on itself, creating an unimaginably powerful gravitational pull. A black hole's gravity is so strong that nothing can escape from it, not even light, so it can't actually be seen. Some scientists think that in the heart of a black hole, the laws of space and time as we know them no longer exist. In effect, something that's sucked into a black hole disappears from this universe.

This computer image shows a black hole's gravity sucking in matter from all around.

Deeply dippy

No one knows for sure what causes gravity, but many scientists think that it's the way that space and time curve. Time and space are very difficult to imagine, but they're often compared to a huge rubbery sheet, stretching to infinity. Planets and stars are like tennis balls on the sheet, making it sag where they lie. Everything around them that's near enough will be pulled towards the dip they make. That's how a planet's gravity pulls things towards it.

This picture shows how planets make a dip in space and time. This might be what creates gravity.

As soon as they jump from their plane, gravity pulls these skydivers back down to Earth. They weigh slightly less in the air than on the ground, because they're further from the Earth's centre.

INTERNET LINK
For a link to a website where you can take a trip inside a black hole, go to www.usborne-quicklinks.com

TRAVELS IN TIME

What's the time? By now, it's already a few seconds later than when you started reading this page. Everyone knows that time exists and can be measured, but the way it behaves is more bizarre than you might think.

The fourth dimension

The famous physicist Albert Einstein created a theory that time is another dimension that exists alongside the three dimensions of space around you. Together, he called these four dimensions "spacetime". It is possible to move in any direction in the three dimensions you can see, but you can move only one way through time.

Albert Einstein's theories on space and time revolutionized people's understanding of the strange ways in which these things work.

Space as you see it has three dimensions: up and down, forward and back, and side to side. You can move in any of these directions.

Time is the fourth dimension, which you can only move through forwards. With a clock or watch you can measure how far through time you've travelled.

The flow of time

Any clock will tell you that, say, sixty seconds pass in every minute, and the length of that minute never varies. But it seems that, in the right conditions, the flow of time can change. For instance, gravity creates "bulges" in the fabric of space and time which affect the way time flows, although you normally can't detect its effects.

How time flies

According to Einstein, time speeds up or slows down depending on how fast you travel, although this only becomes noticeable at extremely high speeds. Imagine you went on a year-long trip around the universe, moving at just below light speed (300,000km or 186,000 miles per second). One year would pass for you, but several would pass on Earth. Since humans can't travel at such speeds, no one has ever directly observed this effect. But mathematical equations show that it must be true.

INTERNET LINK
For a link to a website that demonstrates the strange effects of light-speed travel, go to www.usborne-quicklinks.com

Time travel: fact or fiction?

Everyone thinks that journeying through time to the past or the future is something that only happens in movies and books. But it might actually be possible, through a wormhole – a tunnel through spacetime linking one point in the universe to another one elsewhere. Unfortunately, scientists don't know if wormholes are real, and even if they are, it would be impossible for anyone to use them. But for now, they're the nearest thing to a genuine time machine that humans are aware of.

In theory, wormholes could allow you to travel between any two points in either time or space.

Normally, two points in the vastness of spacetime would be much too far apart to travel between.

Einstein thought that spacetime is curved. If this is true, and most experts believe it is, the distance between the two points could be shorter than it seems.

Shortcuts called wormholes would allow you to travel between the two points. Wormholes might exist in the heart of black holes, but there's no way of finding out yet.

UNDER PRESSURE

Pressure is everywhere. Right now, the Earth's atmosphere is pressing on you from all around. There's pressure inside your body, too, helping it to keep its shape.

Getting jiggly

Pressure isn't just things pressing together, it's what happens when molecules jiggle about. The molecules of a gas or liquid in an enclosed space naturally move about. They bounce off the walls of the container, pressing outwards in every direction as they do so. If the space becomes more limited, they collide more often and the pressure on the walls increases.

The molecules of gas in a jar move around randomly, bouncing off each other and the container.

If the gas is squeezed into a smaller space, the molecules become closer together and collide more, applying more pressure on the jar's walls.

The heart creates pressure to pump blood around the body. This image shows its intricate, root-like system of vessels, through which the blood flows.

Standing firm

Liquid and gas molecules under pressure can generate enough force to make soft things feel solid. It's pressurized water in plants' stems that makes them stand firm and upright, and pressurized air and blood in our bodies that help to keep us from becoming floppy bags of bones and goo.

Atmospheric pressure

The air in Earth's atmosphere presses on you from every direction with surprising strength. In fact, the weight of air pressing down over one square metre of the Earth is heavier than a large elephant. So why doesn't it crush you? The answer is that the fluids in your body push outwards with a force that's equal to the force caused by the air pressure outside it. These two forces cancel each other out.

174

Hurricanes are fierce, swirling masses of wind, rain and lightning, which form in areas of very low air pressure over the sea. Some, like this one, are huge enough to be photographed from space by satellites.

Pressure and weather

Enormous masses of air constantly rise and fall all over the world, creating areas of low or high air pressure beneath them. We don't see them, but we feel their effects. Pressure changes are the driving force behind most of Earth's weather, especially extreme weather like hurricanes and tornadoes.

A tornado forms when huge differences in air pressure cause air to start spinning in a tight, funnel-shaped formation.

It extends down, causing massive damage when it touches the ground. Tornadoes hurl cars and buildings around like toys.

INTERNET LINK
For a link to a website where you can see the effects of pressure beneath the ocean, go to www.usborne-quicklinks.com

Down in the deep

Like air, water applies pressure to everything it surrounds. Divers have to be specially equipped in the deep sea, as the pressure of water around them could easily crush their lungs. Creatures that live in the ocean depths have a startling way to deal with these extreme conditions. The natural pressure inside their bodies is so high that they literally explode if they're brought to the surface.

This scuba diver is breathing air from pressurized tanks. The air is kept at the same pressure as the surrounding water, so his lungs don't collapse.

GOOD VIBRATIONS

Everyone knows how to make sounds. Try humming: you can hear the noise, but you can probably feel something in your throat too. That's your vocal cords vibrating, and they do that because all sounds are made by vibration.

Making waves

Every sound, from the slightest rustle to the most earsplitting roar, is a wave of energy made up of tiny, vibrating particles. The energy transfers from particle to particle until it reaches your ears. Sound waves can travel through gases, liquids and solids, but not through a vacuum. That's why the emptiness of space is completely silent.

The more high-pitched the sound, the closer together the vibrations are. A sound's frequency (the number of sound waves per second) is measured in Hertz (Hz).

A high-pitched sound, such as a whistle, has a high frequency.

A low-pitched sound, such as a tuba, has a low frequency.

The height of the peaks (tops) and depth of the troughs (bottoms) of a sound wave is its amplitude, which shows how loud it is. Loudness is measured in decibels (dB).

A soft sound has a small amplitude.

A loud sound has a large amplitude.

Blue whales can make noises up to a deafening 188dB, louder than any other living thing. The sound waves can be heard thousands of kilometres away through the water.

Sound in a hurry

In air, sound waves move at more than 1,000km (621 miles) per hour. A person running at that speed could cross three soccer fields in a second. But sound travels even more speedily in liquids and solids, because their particles are closer together. In fact, sound carries five times more quickly through water than through air, and 15 times more quickly through steel.

INTERNET LINK
For a link to a website where you can listen to whale sounds, go to
www.usborne-quicklinks.com

The speed of sound

Light moves more quickly than sound, which is why you always see lightning before you hear the thunder it makes, never the other way round. If something starts to travel more quickly than the speed of sound (331.3m, or 1087ft, per second), it's said to be going at supersonic speed. As a supersonic aircraft flies, it squashes the air in front. This is released behind the plane as a shock wave, which makes a tremendous boom.

The misty "egg" in this unique image is actually a mass of air molecules being shaken by shock waves behind a supersonic plane. It's incredibly hard to capture this effect, as it only exists for a moment. This picture was taken from an aircraft carrier in the sea.

A resounding success

You may have heard people say that opera singers can shatter a glass just by singing. This is true, but it's not just to do with the loudness of the sound – it's an effect called resonance. Everything in the universe is vibrating just a little, at its own frequency. If a sound wave matches this rate of vibration it causes resonance, making the object vibrate very strongly and maybe even shaking it to pieces.

Sound weapons

Although we don't think of it as being dangerous, sound can make a surprisingly effective weapon. Scientists are developing weapons which fire "sound bullets" of around 140dB. Any sounds over 120dB are painful to humans, so the bullets, which are actually very concentrated sound waves, can easily put their target out of action.

A sound is made in the end of the weapon, and amplified by a series of crystal wafers as it passes through the tube.

Crystal wafer

When it leaves the tube, the sound wave is extremely loud, but the person it's aimed at is the only one who can hear it.

SOUNDS OF SILENCE

What's described as sound is generally only what people can hear. But there's a world of noise around you that you can't hear at all.

INTERNET LINK
For a link to a website with animations and activities about sound waves, echoes and ultrasound, go to **www.usborne-quicklinks.com**

Hidden noise

The sounds that human ears can detect measure between about 20 and 20,000 Hertz. Higher-pitched sounds are called ultrasound, and ones with lower pitches are called infrasound or subsonic sound. Humans can't hear these, but some other creatures can. For instance, elephants take shelter long before a storm starts, because they can detect the low rumble of distant thunder much sooner than humans. They also communicate with infrasound calls.

Here's how the range of sounds humans can detect compares to those of some other creatures.

25,000–100,000Hz – bat squeaks

40,000Hz – upper limit of dogs' hearing

20,000Hz – upper limit of human hearing

300–3,000Hz – human speech

20Hz – lower limit of human hearing

17–20Hz – blue whale calls

12–35Hz – elephant calls

Bouncing sound

When a sound wave bounces off something, it makes an echo – a repeat of the original sound. Certain animals use the echoes from the sounds they make to find their way around, a technique called echo location.

Echoes from bats' high-pitched squeaks tell them where to find tasty moths to eat.

Baby booms

The ability of sound waves to travel through different substances and bounce back can be used to build up pictures of things you can't see or measure easily. Images made by bouncing ultrasound waves are mostly used in hospitals, to look at unborn babies inside their mothers.

Today's ultrasound scanners are so sophisticated, they can show if an unborn baby is smiling or frowning. This baby is curled up and fast asleep.

See beneath the sea

Ships use ultrasound waves to find out the depth of the ocean in a particular spot, or to see the seabed's shape. This method, called sonar, can also be used to find shipwrecks in the murky depths.

The computer image below shows ridges and valleys beneath the sea. A ship sends out ultrasound waves and measures how long it takes for them to bounce back from the ocean floor. It takes thousands of sound waves bounced off different spots to make an image like this.

Ghostbusting

Although very low infrasound is beyond the human range of hearing, its vibrations seem to have weird effects. Some places where people claimed to feel the presence of ghosts have turned out to be "haunted" by infrasound, which was tricking their brains into making them feel nervous and afraid.

Infrasound sometimes causes people's vision to become blurry, making them see shadowy, ghost-like shapes.

THE HEAT IS ON

You can't see them moving, but the molecules of all solids, liquids or gases are never still. Heat is energy that passes from the vibrating or spinning molecules of an object to anything cooler.

Molecules on the move

When something is heated, it's said to gain more internal energy, which makes its molecules vibrate more quickly and push each other further apart. So, most things grow or swell as they're heated, and shrink as they cool down. The Eiffel Tower in Paris, France, is actually 15cm (5.9in) taller on the hottest days of the year, because it expands in the sun.

Turning up the heat makes molecules become excited. They move more quickly, and spread further apart.

When a substance cools down, its molecules start to vibrate more slowly, moving closer together.

Feeling the heat

Heat is always on the move between hotter and cooler areas, and it has three different ways of getting around. It spreads outwards as infrared radiation, invisible waves given out by every object in the universe. It travels from one part of a substance to another part by conduction: metals conduct heat well, but the best conductor of all is diamond. In air and liquid, heat spreads by convection, which makes it rise and sink in a constant loop.

Heat at the bottom of this lava lamp causes molecules of solid wax to spread out, turning the wax into a liquid. Convection makes the wax flow up, then down, the lamp.

Seeing with heat

Pictures taken by infrared cameras, like this one of a baboon, show patterns of colour based on an object's hot and cold areas. Since infrared cameras can "see" heat, they can detect objects that are hidden behind or inside something else, or in complete darkness. They can also show us details that normal light alone wouldn't reveal.

Letting off steam

If you make a liquid hot enough, it starts to boil – that is, it turns into a gas. Normally, water bubbles and turns to steam as it boils, and this energy loss keeps it from getting any hotter. But if for some reason bubbles can't form, the water's temperature rises and rises until it's beyond the normal boiling temperature, and it becomes superheated. If something acts as a trigger, all the stored heat energy is unleashed in one huge burst. In some parts of the world, the power of superheating has created explosive columns of water called geysers.

INTERNET LINK
For a link to a website with surprising infrared images and infrared facts, go to www.usborne-quicklinks.com

Infrared imaging displays this baboon's hottest parts in red and yellow, and her coolest areas in blue and purple. Normally, you could only learn information like this by touch.

The geysers in this photograph show superheating's mighty force. Water in underground chambers is superheated by hot rock surrounding it, before erupting in violent, boiling sprays.

COLD SCIENCE

If you have a freezer in your home, you'll know it's useful to be able to cool things down. But what about if you make them colder still? Just how cold can something get, and what happens to it?

Feeling the cold

Really low temperatures can be both helpful and harmful to living things. Extreme cold normally kills living cells and tissue, but under the right conditions, it can be used to preserve them. For instance, blood and body organs can be kept in a laboratory in very cold liquid nitrogen, then thawed and used in operations.

Frozen life isn't confined to a lab, though. Some animals have a high level of a natural antifreeze called glycol inside them that allows their bodies to chill completely and become death-like during the winter. In spring, they thaw out and wake up as if they'd simply been taking a nap.

Wood frogs hibernate during the harsh winter. They bury themselves in icy pond mud, and their bodies freeze solid.

Freezing would kill most animals, but the frogs' unique body chemistry allows them to revive in the spring with no ill effects.

How low can you go?

The lowest naturally occurring temperature recorded on Earth is -89°C (-128°F), in the Antarctic. That's extremely cold, although not nearly the coldest temperature in the universe. One of Neptune's moons, Triton, has a surface temperature of a chilling -235°C (-455°F), but even that isn't the coldest known place. Radiation left behind from its creation allowed scientists to measure the overall temperature of the universe itself – an astonishing -270.42°C (-518.76°F). That's almost as cold as you can possibly get.

Absolutely freezing

The lowest theoretical temperature that could exist is -273.15°C (-523.67°F), also known as absolute zero. Something cooled to this level can't get any colder, because its internal energy is at a minimum. Scientists think that reaching absolute zero might be impossible, although they have cooled atoms to within a millionth of a degree of it using laser pulses to slow down their movement.

Laser beams apply a very tiny force to any atoms they touch. If you shine lasers on an atom from many different angles, it can be made to move more slowly. No one has yet stopped an atom completely, though.

That's super cool!

Helium gas cooled to about -269°C (-516°F) turns to a liquid. But at a few fractions of a degree above absolute zero, it becomes something called a superfluid. Superfluids are unique because all their atoms travel at the same speed and in the same direction, instead of randomly as in normal liquids. This makes superfluids incredibly smooth-flowing: they can move without friction through the tiniest of gaps, and even up the sides of containers.

INTERNET LINK
For a link to a website where you can see what happens to atoms at low temperatures, go to www.usborne-quicklinks.com

Superconductors

At around -253°C (-423°F), some materials become superconductors, which means they allow electricity to pass freely through them without resistance. So, unlike normal conductors, they waste no energy as heat while current flows through them. In fact, they can conduct electric current for years with next to no energy loss. They also produce exceptionally powerful magnetic fields.

Electric current flows easily through superconducting materials like this, creating a magnetic field strong enough to make a metal disk float above it. The glowing mist is liquid nitrogen, which keeps the material cool enough to be a superconductor.

CURRENT AFFAIRS

You probably know already that electricity has the power to light a room, make a TV work, and so on. But you might not know that this power exists inside everything.

Feeling energetic

People often describe electricity as energy, but that's not quite right: actually, electricity carries energy. Energy from electricity can be gained or lost. For instance, it is lost when a lightbulb changes it into light and heat. But while this conversion is going on, electricity still continues to flow through the wire. So, the energy and the electricity itself must be separate things.

This lightbulb turns electrical energy into light and heat energy.

Battery

Wire

Light and heat energy

Lightbulb

Electrons with energy

Electrons without energy

If you connect a battery and a lightbulb with a loop of wire, you've made an electrical circuit. Electricity flows through the circuit and the bulb uses the energy it carries.

Electrifying atoms

The answer to what electricity really is lies inside an atom, where protons and electrons hold positive and negative electrical charges. Normally there is the same amount of each, but if atoms lose or gain electrons, they can become positively or negatively charged (and are called ions).

Electricity is a result of the way that charged particles behave. Because they are charged, there is an electric force between them. Any charge produces an invisible effect around it called an electric field. Another charge that strays into this field feels an electric force.

Electrical fields cause charged particles to push and pull. Those with the same charge repel each other; those with opposite charges are attracted.

Charging ahead

Charges on the move are called electrical current, and this is what carries electrical energy through a wire. An electrical current always needs something to flow through, and something to move it. Batteries, for instance, act like pumps to move charges along.

Charges move very slowly: in fact, sometimes they don't travel at all, they just jiggle about. So how can a light come on right away when you flick a switch? It's because there are already charged atoms in the wires between the switch and the bulb. Think of the current working in the same way as a wheel – if you give it a push, the whole thing is instantly affected. You don't have to wait for the movement to travel from one part of the wheel to another.

Electricity flows with no resistance through the bundles of wire in superconducting cables like this one, so no energy is wasted.

INTERNET LINK
For a link to a website with interactive animations about electricity, circuits and more, go to www.usborne-quicklinks.com

Good conduct

A substance that allows charge to move through it easily is called a conductor. Metals are really good conductors, but materials like wood and plastic barely conduct at all. Whether something conducts or not is all to do with the properties of its electrons and the way they can or can't move.

A conductor is like a pipe full of water. The current flows freely between atoms in a moving "sea" of electrons.

An insulator is like a pipe full of ice. Its electrons are fixed in place, so current can barely flow.

Meeting resistance

Almost every substance, even a conductor, has a little resistance to electricity flowing through it. Resistance causes energy to be lost – in fact, about 10% of electrical energy is wasted as it flows through wires, usually as heat. Resistance isn't all bad, though, as it's what allows electric fires and toasters to work.

185

TAKING CHARGE

When electrical charges flow, they make an electric current. But if they have nowhere to go to, they build up instead. Eventually, they may be unleashed as a powerful spark.

Building up charge

Normally, a material's atoms are electrically neutral, which means that they have equal positive and negative electrical charges. But if you rub together two insulators (materials that don't conduct electricity well), some electrons will be transferred from one to the other, making one negative and the other positive. This build-up of charge is called static electricity, and the energy stored by separating this charge is measured by voltage: the greater the amount of charge separated, the greater the voltage.

A spark of static electricity can jump between any two objects with opposite charges – in this case, the tips of a pair of nails.

Electric body

Static electricity is what you sometimes experience if your feet build up charge as you walk across a carpeted room then touch a metal doorknob. As the charge from your body leaps to the doorknob, you may hear a crackling sound and even see a spark. This can be up to several thousand volts, but you rarely feel more than a sting.

Static cling

If static can exist between any insulators in contact with each other, you might wonder why you don't see sparks every time you pick up a book or a pencil. In fact, the amount of charge depends on the materials and the amount of touching surface area between them. The flatter the objects, the more surface contact, and the more the voltage increases.

Some materials give up electrons and become charged more readily than others. For instance, hair gives up electrons easily, and plastic is better at gaining them.

Using a plastic comb to bend water may look like magic, but it's easy if you run the comb through your hair first. This charges the comb with electrons, and the water is then attracted to the comb's negative charge.

186

A model plane is being used to test how real aircraft react to lightning strikes. This "lightning" is a high-voltage spark, generated in a lab.

Sparks in the sky

Lightning is the big, bold brother of the spark that jumps between your hand and a doorknob, and, like your skin and the knob, it's caused by an attraction between oppositely charged things. If ice and rain rub together in a cloud, they create a build-up of separated charges in the cloud's top and bottom. The negative charges in the bottom are attracted to positive charges in the ground, and electrons start to flow between the two, creating a path through the sky. This path is what lightning leaps along.

INTERNET LINK
For a link to a website where you can watch animations about lightning, circuits and electricity, go to www.usborne-quicklinks.com

Sprites and jets

Every so often, lightning is generated from the upper part of a storm cloud instead of the lower part, and its unusually intense electrical field creates a spectacular light show. It might appear as a massive, jellyfish-shaped burst of red light called a sprite, which shoots up into the air high above the storm, or as a jet – a flash of blue light spreading upwards at up to 100km (62 miles) per second. But very few people have seen or photographed these rare, unpredictable sights, because they happen so far up.

Lightning in the lab

In the late 19th century, a scientist named Nikola Tesla revolutionized the way people thought about and used electricity. One of his many electrical creations was a device to harness the extreme power of lightning inside a laboratory. He named his invention, which transforms opposite charges into brief pulses of powerful electricity, a Tesla coil.

Here, a scientist sees the shocking effects of a Tesla coil. Although he looks worried, he is protected by a Faraday cage, a metal suit designed to keep bolts of electricity away from whatever's inside it.

THE BODY ELECTRIC

In the story of Frankenstein, a monster was brought to life with electricity. But that's not as far-fetched as it sounds – electricity in our bodies is what allows us to move, think and react to the world around us.

Human computers

In a way, people are like living computers – they use electricity to sort complex information and react to instructions from outside. Everything you sense is translated into electrical signals that travel between your body parts and your brain. The tiny cells which your body is made of act like batteries, generating electricity as charged atoms, called ions, move through them.

Brains and chips

The brain is more complex than the most sophisticated machine on Earth. Inside it, over 10 billion nerve cells, called neurons, are constantly exchanging information. Scientists have recently created an electronic "neuro-chip", a computer chip which strengthens the pulses of electricity from neurons and transfers them to a computer for processing. This will improve scientists' knowledge of how the brain works, making it easier to treat brain diseases.

Here you can see a nerve cell that's been grown on an electronic sensor chip. Each chip is only about the size of a pinhead, but can record huge amounts of information about how nerves respond to things.

Keeping pace

Have you ever wondered what keeps your heart beating? It's a series of regular electrical jolts from a tiny clump of cells inside your heart called pacemakers. They often die or wear out with age, but their owner can be given a new lease of life by being fitted with an artificial electrical pacemaker. The batteries need changing every ten or so years, though, and can be damaged easily by strong magnetic fields.

Recently, scientists have found a way to change the flow of substances in and out of the heart's cells by adding a chemical instruction called a gene. The altered flow creates a negative electrical charge in the heart's ordinary cells, turning them into new pacemaker cells.

This X-ray image shows an electronic pacemaker keeping a person's heartbeat regular. Scientists are finding new ways to repair the heart's cells to make bulky implants like this a thing of the past.

INTERNET LINK
For a link to a website where you can take a 3-D tour of a brain, go to **www.usborne-quicklinks.com**

Chain of command

Just as a computer reacts when you click on a mouse button, your body can translate actions into responses. The central nervous system, made of your brain and spinal cord, interprets information from your senses and sends commands through chains of neurons. And, just like a computer, it runs on electricity.

When a neuron is excited by sensations such as touch, it generates a tiny electrical pulse. At the same time, chemicals called neurotransmitters are released in the cell.

The electrical pulse travels through the body to the neuron's thin, finger-like ends, in the spinal cord. All neurons almost, but not quite, touch the ends of the next one.

The neurotransmitters help the pulse to jump to the next neuron. This neuron then passes the pulse on to another, until the message reaches the brain.

MIGHTY MAGNETS

Magnetism is an invisible force which certain materials can create, and which most things are affected by. Planet Earth is a magnet, and you're magnetic too.

Here, magnetic powder is being used to dust for fingerprints. Some of the powder sticks to grease in the prints, and the rest is lifted away by a magnet.

Pole position

A free-moving magnet always swivels to point in a north-south direction. The parts of a magnet which control this attraction are its north and south poles. Even if you cut a magnet into many pieces, each one will have two poles.

Identical magnetic poles always push each other away.

Opposite magnetic poles always pull each other together.

Getting magnetic

If you've ever tried sticking something to a refrigerator door, you'll know that some things are magnetic and some aren't. A magnet is anything with its own magnetic field – a force which affects other magnetic things around it. Every molecule of a magnet is like a tiny magnet itself, and all its poles point the same way. Some materials, such as iron, can become magnets for a short time when placed in a magnetic field, which makes the magnetic poles inside them line up together.

Iron filings scattered around a magnet always line up in the shape of its magnetic field, as this picture shows.

INTERNET LINK
For a link to a website where you can
take a virtual tour of an MRI machine,
go to www.usborne-quicklinks.com

Seeing with magnets

MRI (magnetic resonance imaging) is a way of using magnets to see inside the body. The patient lies in a tube which gives out a powerful magnetic field, and radio waves are passed through the body. This causes some of the patient's body atoms to change their movement. Only about three in every million atoms are affected, but that's enough information for a computer to generate amazing, detailed images.

This MRI scan of a brain has revealed a tumour on the left side.

Magnetic Earth

The centre of the Earth is made of solid iron surrounded by a layer of liquid iron. As the Earth spins, this fluid metal swirls and generates a magnetic field around the planet, making it act like a giant magnetic bar. A compass needle always points north because its poles are attracted to the poles of the Earth's magnetic field.

Some animals have tiny crystals of a magnetic substance called magnetite inside their bodies, so they can detect the Earth's magnetic field. This astonishing "sixth sense" acts like a natural compass, guiding animals around the world on journeys of thousands of kilometres to have babies or find food.

Living magnets

When you think of magnets, you usually think of metals. But solid things with lots of water in them, including animals and humans, can be magnetic too. Water is diamagnetic, which means the electrons in its atoms, which all have their own magnetic fields, always repel magnetism from outside. Although the diamagnetic force is about 100,000 times weaker than normal magnetism, if you have a strong enough magnetic field you can use diamagnetism to make living things float.

If a frog is placed in a tube with a strong magnetic field, the electrons in the frog's atoms will try to push against the outside force.

The frog will start to float as its charged electrons repel the surrounding magnetic field. Even a human could float in a strong enough field.

191

ELECTROMAGNETISM

You might think from its name alone that electromagnetism has something to do with electricity and magnetism, and you'd be absolutely right. They have many features in common, which is why they're often described together as a single force.

A versatile force

Electromagnetism is one of the most important forces in the universe. As well as controlling how electricity and magnetism work, it holds together the atoms that everything is made of.

You'll also see the word "electromagnetic" used to describe some types of rays. That's because the tiny blips of electromagnetic energy known as photons are also what make rays of light, microwaves, and the whole range of energy waves known as the electromagnetic spectrum.

Electromagnetic forces inside atoms create contact forces. These keep objects from merging together, for example, stopping the atoms in this hand from merging with the surface it's touching.

Electrons whizz around an atom's nucleus (middle) in areas known as shells. The further from the nucleus an electron's shell is, the more energy it has. Electrons can move from shell to shell, gaining or losing energy as they go. The energy exists in little "packets" called photons.

If an electron moves nearer to the nucleus, as in this diagram, it loses energy and gives out a photon. An electron moves to an outer shell when it gains energy from a photon. These moving photons are electromagnetic waves.

Atom

Nucleus

Electron shell

Electron

Photon

Making contact

The atoms that make up all objects are mostly empty space, so what keeps two things from merging together when they touch? The answer is electromagnetism. Electromagnetic (EM) forces cause electrons in an atom's outer shell to repel electrons in other atoms. This creates an invisible barrier between solid things which we experience as their hard surface.

Let's stick together

Electromagnetic forces don't just keep solid things solid, they also play a vital part in joining atoms together to make molecules. Usually, an atom has an equal number of positive protons and negative electrons, which means the charges are balanced, making the atom electrically neutral. Since all the charges are cancelled out, in theory it shouldn't be possible for atoms to attract each other and form molecules. But when atoms get close enough, the EM force allows this to happen.

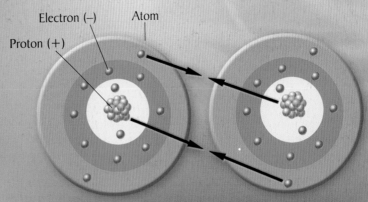

Electron (–)   Atom
Proton (+)

The electromagnetic force allows the negatively charged electrons of one atom to attract the positively charged protons of another, so the atoms can stick together.

Making magnets

Since electricity and magnetism are so closely linked, you can use one to create the other. Coiled wire with an electric current running through it generates a magnetic field, and if you put materials such as iron in the coils, they become electromagnets – magnets you can turn on and off by changing the current. These are used in all kinds of gadgets, such as phones and modems, and also to create extra-smooth movement. Scientists are developing ways to launch spacecraft more easily using maglev (**mag**netic **lev**itation) tracks, which avoid the slowing effect of friction by making the rocket float.

When the coils in this electromagnetic launch track are electrified, they generate a powerful magnetic field, shown in red in this computer image. The field repels magnets underneath the rocket and it floats above the track, allowing for a smoother, faster launch.

INTERNET LINK
For a link to a website with electromagnet activities, go to www.usborne-quicklinks.com

The whole universe is tingling with energy waves. Light is a group of energy waves you can see, but it is actually one part of a great range of waves that are invisible, known as the electromagnetic (EM) spectrum.

Electromagnetic waves

All EM waves zip through space at the speed of light. Like sound waves, EM waves can travel through solids, liquids and gases, but they can pass through the empty space of a vacuum too. The diagram below shows how EM waves can be grouped by their wavelength, that is, the distance between the top of one wave and the next, and their frequency, which is how many waves pass by in a second.

Gamma rays and X-rays have a short wavelength and high frequency.

The electromagnetic spectrum

- Gamma rays
- X-rays
- UV light
- Visible light
- Infrared light
- Microwaves
- Radio waves

Microwaves and radio waves have a long wavelength and low frequency.

World wide waves

These mysterious glowing shapes are the Large Magellanic Cloud, which lies thousands of light years away in space. Like many space objects, this galaxy gives off radio waves. These are the longest EM waves, whose wavelength makes them good at piercing our cloudy atmosphere. Astronomers use huge, dish-shaped aerials to detect radio waves that come to Earth from space, and they use the information to build up pictures like this one. Radio waves are also more widely used for sending TV, radio and mobile phone signals around the world.

Radio signals from space are turned into images, like this one of a galaxy called the Large Magellanic Cloud.

Microwave meals

When you warm up your lunch in a microwave oven, you are using EM waves. Microwaves, like all EM waves, are made of quick-changing electric and magnetic fields. As the fields switch direction, water molecules in the food absorb their energy and spin around like the magnetic needle on a compass. As its molecules move more and more quickly, the food heats up, and cooks.

Intense microwaves make water molecules in food spin around millions of times every second.

X-ray vision

X-rays can show views that usually can't be seen. These short, high-energy EM waves can easily pass through some materials that block out light. In X-ray photos, like this one of a snake, the X-rays beam through skin and flesh as effortlessly as light through a window, but bone is dense enough to block them, so it shows up as white.

This portrait is thought to have been painted by the Italian artist Giorgione.

This X-ray photo of the portrait shows a hand that has been painted over.

INTERNET LINK
For a link to a website where you can take a guided tour of the electromagnetic spectrum, go to www.usborne-quicklinks.com

This X-ray photo shows a snake that had a frog for dinner. The X-rays even pass through the frog, showing us the shape of its bones. Bone contains a metal called calcium which soaks up X-rays. This is why the bones show up as solid areas in the photograph.

THE LIGHT FANTASTIC

Light is a form of travelling
energy that can be seen.
Many of the things that are
known about light come
from watching the
strange or spectacular
effects it produces.

Shadow play

Light travels so quickly
that you can't see it
moving at all. We know
it does move, though,
because its movement can
be blocked. Objects block
light by soaking up its
energy, or reflecting it back.

Where light is blocked, a shadow
forms behind the object blocking
it. The more light that is blocked,
the darker the shadow that appears.

Light travels in straight lines called rays.
You can sometimes see this when sunbeams
stream through clouds, or into a dusty room.

This spectacular sight is a total eclipse of the Sun, when the Moon
passes in front of the Sun, blocking out its light. The white glow is
a super-hot layer of gas that surrounds the Sun, called the corona.

Bouncing back

Most objects reflect some or all of the light rays
hitting them. Dark objects soak up most of the
light that hits them, but mirrors and white
objects reflect back nearly all of it. Mirrors are
extremely smooth, so light rays that hit them
bounce straight back to the viewer, reflecting
an image. On a microscopic scale, white
surfaces are much rougher, so the reflected
light rays are scattered, and no image is seen.

Mirrors reflect light rays
straight back to the viewer.

White objects scatter light
rays in many directions.

196

Lightning speed

Thunder is the sound made by lightning, but it often takes a few seconds to hear the thunder after the lightning, even though they happen at the same time. This shows how much more quickly light travels than sound. In fact, light is the fastest thing we know: it moves at 300,000km (186,000 miles) per second through empty space. A ray of light could circle the Earth seven-and-a-half times in a second.

Light takes next to no time to travel 1km, but sound takes three seconds. To find a storm's distance (in km) count the seconds from lightning to thunder and divide by three (for miles, divide by five).

Bending light

Substances that block light are called opaque. Others, like glass or water, are transparent: they let light through. Substances that let some light through are called translucent.

Scientists study the way light moves through substances to learn more about it. When light moves from air into a denser substance, such as glass or water, it slows down. If it hits the substance at an angle it also changes direction. This is why objects seen through water look distorted, or seem closer than they really are.

Insect appears to be here

Insect in the line of fire

Archer fish hunt insects they spot above the water. They know that their line of sight is distorted if they view their prey from an angle, and have developed a trick to make up for it...

The archer fish swims beneath its prey so that its line of sight is true. It then spits a jet of water, knocking the unlucky insect off its perch. Then it's lunchtime.

As light shines through these glass prisms, it changes direction, and splits up into the colours you can see here.

INTERNET LINK
For a link to an animated website with loads of light facts and activities, go to www.usborne-quicklinks.com

MAKING LIGHT WORK

Light can do more than let you see: scientists have harnessed its great speed to send messages around the world in the blink of an eye, and have focused its energy in the power and precision of laser beams.

Light messenger

When you're sending an email, or chatting to a friend on the other side of the world, the chances are that your message is being carried by fibre-optic cables. Fibre-optic cables send messages coded as pulses of light. The light is fired by a laser and carried along the inside of incredibly pure strands of glass or plastic called optical fibres.

Fibre-optic cables contain thousands of optical fibres, thinner than a hair, yet stronger than steel. Compared to copper wires, fibre-optics last longer, can carry many more phone calls, and aren't affected by electricity, so you can't get a "crossed wire".

Light travels in straight lines. To keep it moving along through a bending fibre, it's bounced off a mirror-like layer of cladding.

These glowing strands are optical fibres. A single fibre can carry a million phone calls at once, in the form of pulses of light.

Laser light

The shining surfer below is showing off just one of the many uses of lasers. White light is a mixture of coloured wavelengths spreading out in many directions. Lasers produce bright beams of a single colour, focused in one direction.

The coloured wavelengths in white light spread out in many directions.

Laser light is focused into one intense, bright wave of a single colour.

Lasers are often used in light shows to "paint" pictures on a screen or wall of mist. A computer controls where the beams are fired, and they move so quickly that their tips blur into lines.

INTERNET LINK
For a link to an animated website that shows you all about lasers, go to
www.usborne-quicklinks.com

Straight to the point

The narrowness of laser beams suits them to very precise work. In a CD player, a laser scans thousands of microscopic bumps on the underside of a CD, and electronics turn this information into music. Powerful lasers are used in surgery to act as precise cutting instruments, or to weld human tissue together.

As a CD spins in a player, a laser beam bounces off minuscule bumps on its underside. As each bump whizzes by, a lens picks up a laser signal. The signals are then translated into music.

Laser   Lens

Bump: the lens receives a signal.

No bump: no signal is received.

199

COLOUR

Whether you're painting a picture or choosing a new toothbrush it's easy to take colour for granted. The way you see colour involves the movement of light, the chemicals in an object and the way your eyes and brain work.

Light reflecting from this macaw's feathers carries its dazzling colours to your eyes.

Rainbows show the colours hidden in sunlight. You only see them when the Sun is behind you.

INTERNET LINK
For a link to a website where you can mix colours online, go to
www.usborne-quicklinks.com

Hidden in sunlight

Rainbows are seen when rays of sunlight shine through raindrops, split up and spread out. They show that light, though it looks white, is really a mixture of differently coloured light. These colours are called the visible spectrum. Sometimes the rays also reflect inside the raindrops, producing a second, fainter, rainbow above the first.

Chemical colour

Most objects contain chemicals called pigments, which soak up some of the colours from white light as it hits them. The remaining colours are reflected back to your eyes, and these are the colours you see.

A red feather has pigment which soaks up all the colours in light except red, so only red light reaches your eyes.

200

The mind's eye

Both your eyes and your brain are vital to seeing colour. Inside the back of your eye are thousands of tiny light-sensitive cells called rods and cones. Rods sense the brightness of light and cones sense its colour. There are three types of cone, sensing red, green or blue light, and all colours are seen as mixtures of these three colours. When you look at something, the rods send messages along the optic nerve to tell the brain how bright the object is. The cones send messages about its colour. The brain combines these messages to create an image of what you see.

These light-sensing cells in the human eye are magnified hundreds of times. The thin structures are called rods and the fat ones are called cones.

Colour film

Not all colour is made by pigment. Soap bubbles have a fine double film of oil on their surfaces that splits white light into the colours of the rainbow. These colours reflect off the oil films and interfere with each other. Some colours add together, becoming brighter; others are cancelled out, leaving dark areas.

The colours that swim across bubbles are created as light reflects off oil swirling on their surfaces.

In a different light

Some animals can see colours that can't be seen by humans. Many insects, birds, fish and reptiles can see beyond the violet end of the visible spectrum, into the ultraviolet (UV). Many fruits that look dark to us, such as plums, look bright and inviting in UV, so birds and insects are attracted to them among the much darker-looking leaves.

To human eyes, these silverweed flowers are yellow with no patterns or markings.

To bees, the same flowers have bright UV markings. The patterns lead the bees to the sweet-tasting nectar in the middle of the flower.

OPTICAL ILLUSIONS

You can't always trust your eyes to show you the truth. Optical illusions are visual tricks that surprise your eyes and brains by showing them sights they are unlikely to see in the real world.

Double take

The eyes may see something, but it takes the brain to make sense of what is seen. This is called perception. The pictures on the right can both be perceived in different ways, and this baffles our brains because it wants to decide what it is seeing.

Is this a picture of a vase, or is it two lovers about to kiss?

A young woman looking away or an old lady looking down?

INTERNET LINK
For a link to a website where you can see more optical illusions, and discover how they work, go to www.usborne-quicklinks.com

Seeing in stereo

Stereograms use the way the eyes focus on things to create a 3-D illusion. When your eyes focus on a flat page, they both look at the same point and see pretty much the same thing. The brain decides from this that the page is flat. The stereogram on the left repeats a pattern across the page, but it changes slightly each time. These differences fool the brain into thinking it is seeing a 3-D object rather than a flat page, and it joins the patterns together to make a 3-D picture.

To see the hidden 3-D image, let your eyes relax and cross slightly and focus a little way *beyond* the page.

202

Dizzy spells

The wheels above seem to be
spinning – unless you look at a
wheel directly. The illusion works
because the brain concentrates mainly on what the eyes
are focusing on. At the edge of your vision you notice
bright things more quickly than dark things, so you see
the light parts of the wheels first. This delay creates
an illusion of movement from dark to light areas.

The only cogs
turning are in your
brain... If the illusion
above makes you feel dizzy or
unwell, please turn to another page.

Sometimes there is a gap between seeing and
perceiving, but once the brain has made up
its mind it tends to stick with its decision. At
first, the picture above may look like a jumble
of spots, but it soon becomes very hard *not*
to see a dalmatian dog sniffing the ground.

Squares A and B are really the same colour.
Go to **www.usborne-quicklinks.com** to see
the proof. The brain has different areas to
deal with perceiving colour and shade.
Here, the brain is busier working out the
colour of square B than its exact shade.

These squares seem to bulge but their
edges line up straight. The way the smaller
squares are arranged makes the corner
angles of the larger squares seem sharper
than they are, so their edges look slanted.

COMPUTERS EVERYWHERE

Scientists are constantly developing faster and cleverer computers. The computers of the future will be built into houses, cars and even clothes. People will be able to use them wherever they go.

Fast worker

A super-fast computer has been developed that uses light, not electricity, to process 8 billion instructions in one second. It contains 256 lasers performing calculations at light-speed and is 1,000 times faster than the computers you use at home or school. The very earliest electronic computers, made in the 1940s, could only process around 5,000 instructions per second.

This laser keyboard can be beamed onto any surface. You can use it like a real keyboard, even though the only thing you touch is a beam of light.

Clip-on computers

Active badges – nametag-sized computers that are pinned onto clothes – can be used as trackers to trace where you are in a building and who you have stopped to talk to. Future badges will also interact with their surroundings in a way that is personalized to you. An automated voice in every room you enter could greet you by name and every computer you sit at could automatically reset itself to your preferences.

INTERNET LINK
For a link to a website about testing new technology, go to
www.usborne-quicklinks.com

The computers of the future might look like this. As you walk around a building, a computer pinned to your clothes could be storing and sending out information about you.

E-paper

Computerized paper could bring books and magazines to life. It would be flexible and feel like normal paper, but a single page would hold lots of books and articles, illustrated by video clips and animations. Slim, book-sized display panels have already been developed. You can download newspapers and magazines onto them, then fold – or even roll – them up and put them away.

This ultra-thin computer screen folds like a book.

Smartly dressed

Mobile computers already exist in the form of laptops and handhelds, but soon people might be wearing computers on their bodies. "Smart clothing" is made of a type of fabric that combines cloth with computer technology. This could let you make telephone calls from your shirt, or even surf the internet from your coat.

This small computer screen is attached to the hood of a raincoat. It brings up information about the wearer's surroundings.

Invisible computers

In the future, your life might be monitored by computers that are built into your home, school or office. They would be built in so well that you wouldn't even notice they were there. The computers would work out what you wanted them to do by monitoring your voice, gestures and expressions, using sensors such as cameras and microphones.

CAUGHT IN THE NET

Can you imagine a world without email, websites or instant messaging? Just 15 years ago, email was only used by the army and scientists, and the World Wide Web hadn't even been invented. Today, 500 million people all over the world use the internet for entertainment, communication and information.

Cold connection

Internet connections can be installed into almost any household product. You can already buy an Internet Fridge, which has a computer on its door, a digital calendar to track your schedule and a camcorder for leaving video messages. You can use the fridge to email, surf the Web, download MP3 music, play DVDs and watch TV. It also tracks food supplies and will warn you when you're running low on anything.

The purple lines on this globe show internet connections in the United States – the country with the most internet users. In 2004, over 200 million people in the US had internet connections at home.

Speed freak

Waiting and waiting for audio and video files to download could be a thing of the past now that researchers have come up with Fast TCP. This is an internet connection that is 153,000 times faster than a modem. With Fast TCP, an entire movie can be downloaded in under five seconds.

Space net

Soon, the internet could link to outer space. Information from space probes and astronauts could be sent to Earth using the same type of internet communication that you use to send instant messages to your friends. This would make communication between space and Earth over 20,000 times faster than it is today. People would also be able to see clearer images of planets and even go on virtual missions to outer space from the comfort of their living rooms.

Information from machines exploring Mars could be sent to satellites orbiting the planet. The satellites would have an internet link to Earth.

Antennas on Earth would receive the information from the satellites, 20,000 times faster than they do with existing technology.

Cyber criminals

Computers connected to a network can be accessed by criminals called hackers. In many countries, networked computers control important systems, from telecommunications, air traffic controls and water supplies, to dams, power stations and financial services. Even food distribution, healthcare and emergency services are on networks. If thieves or terrorists managed to break into these networks, whole nations could be thrown into chaos. Software companies are constantly writing new security programs to keep one step ahead of the hackers and protect society from disaster.

Some hackers try to write software that enables them to clean out bank accounts or tamper with countries' defence systems. If they are caught breaking into other people's computers, they could be sent to jail.

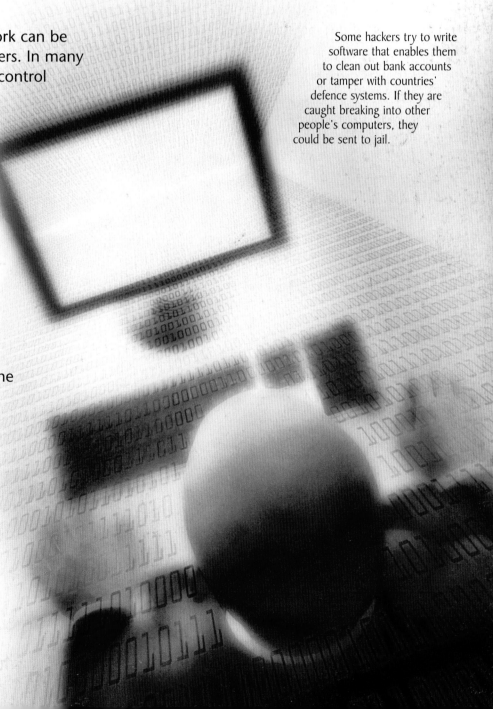

INTERNET LINK
For a link to a website about hackers and internet security, go to
www.usborne-quicklinks.com

THINKING COMPUTERS

Computers can carry out lots of instructions very quickly, but the quickest and most complicated instruction-processing system in the world is the human brain. Researchers are trying to create computers that "think" in a similar way to humans.

Robocup

Every July, soccer teams from all over the world compete in a huge tournament. This may sound like the World Cup, but there is one important difference – the players are all robots, programmed to think like soccer players. They must decide for themselves where to kick the ball and how to work as a team.

The organizers of the robot soccer tournament hope that, by 2050, a team of robots like these will have beaten the world's best human team.

Computer scientist

Researchers have programmed a computer to design laboratory experiments, carry them out, and even interpret the data, all without any human help. The computer controls a robot arm that can do the physical work, like holding test tubes and pouring liquids. Its inventors are hoping that, in the future, the computer will make new scientific discoveries.

Checkmate

In 2003, the world's most advanced chess computer program, X3D Fritz, took on the world's best chess player, Garry Kasparov, for the title of Man-Machine World Champion. The games were played in X3D virtual reality, with the board appearing to float in the air in front of Kasparov. To move the pieces, Kasparov simply told the computer what moves he wanted to make. Four games were played in all. The result? A tie. Kasparov and Fritz won two games each and had to share the title.

Electronic emotion

Jeremiah is a computer program that suffers from mood swings. This interactive virtual head can be downloaded onto a PC, where he will respond to what is happening around him. If nothing is happening, he looks sad, but waving at him will soon bring a smile to his face. Sudden movements surprise him, but when he sees an object that isn't moving, he'll assume it's ignoring him and become angry. He will happily follow a moving object with his eyes, but doing this for too long will make him bored.

This picture shows just some of the moods Jeremiah – an interactive virtual head – can express.

INTERNET LINK

For a link to a website where you can watch Jeremiah, the virtual head, go to **www.usborne-quicklinks.com**

Watching the skies

A team of astronomers has developed a computer program that keeps a constant watch on the sky. Using a network of telescopes linked over the Internet, the program can sift through sky observations, comparing them to previous images of the same region. It can decide whether it has spotted something interesting enough for further study and, if it has, will make more observations. In the future, the program will be able to take live action pictures of any interesting events it has seen and send them to astronomers' mobile phones.

When an asteroid moves across the sky, a telescope could spot it, turn on its video camera...

...and send a live-action picture of the asteroid to an astronomer's mobile phone.

RISE OF THE ROBOTS

Robots are machines that have computers for brains. They are very useful as they can do the dull, repetitive jobs that people don't want to do and the difficult or dangerous jobs that they can't.

Helpful humanoids

Some robots are built to look and act like very helpful humans. Chatty humanoid robots can give out information about events in museums and theme parks. Some can also give directions, make small talk about the weather and fashion, and even ask for a cup of tea. To make them seem even more human, they can be programmed to show moods such as friendliness, fright, curiosity, irritation and boredom.

This humanoid robot can act as a tour guide and interactive information kiosk.

Robot butler

Scientists are developing a robot that will act as a personal assistant. The robot, called Cardea, can already recognize a door, roll up to it and open it with its one arm. Cardea will eventually have three arms, each one with a different attachment. One could carry objects, such as groceries, and another could unscrew jars and bottles.

Cardea currently looks like this...

... but may eventually look like this.

Walking chair

In the future, wheelchairs could be replaced by robot walking chairs. The WL-16 robot has two feet and is strong enough to carry a person. It can walk forwards, backwards and sideways and even go up and down steps. At the moment, it is radio-controlled but its inventors hope to fit it with a joystick that can be controlled by the user.

The WL-16 walks smoothly, even if its user moves about in the chair.

The robot can even carry its user up and down stairs.

Spy snake

Not all robots are designed to look and act like humans – some are based on animals. A snake robot has been developed that can act as a spy, with a video camera and broadcast system. The robot can be dropped from a helicopter onto a battlefield and will wriggle along the ground like a real snake until it reaches its destination. But, unlike a real snake, the robot will keep moving even if it gets damaged.

Wires run through the robot's body, supplying it with power and allowing it to slither along the ground like a snake.

Robot swarm

Tiny robots, the size of insects, could be swarming over the fields and factories of the future. They could be used to carry out checks and repairs inside complex or delicate machinery, to search buildings for chemical and biological weapons, or to locate and disable land mines.

This robot is fitted with a temperature sensor. Future versions could have a chemical sensor, camera, microphone, and communication device. The sweetcorn it is sitting on gives you an idea of just how small it is.

INTERNET LINK
For a link to a website with online activities about designing robots, go to www.usborne-quicklinks.com

SMALL WONDERS

Can you imagine something that is only one millionth of a millimetre long? Using the most powerful microscopes, scientists are able not only to see particles that are this tiny but also to use them to make materials and machines. Using particles in this way is called nanotechnology.

Smart dust

Scientists are developing microscopic devices, the size of a grain of sand, to act as miniature detectives. Called smart dust, the machines could be used to find impurities in drinking water, poisonous gases in the air and even cancerous cells in the human body. Smart dust already exists in the form of tiny sensors that are just millimetres long. They can monitor motion, temperature, and levels of light and radiation.

The pollution-detectors of the future may look like this — tiny machines so small that they would be able to fit through the eye of a needle.

Nanowhiskers

Nanotechnology can be put to use anywhere, even on your clothes. Tiny carbon hairs called nanowhiskers have been invented to help messy eaters stay stain-free. Natural fabrics, like cotton, can be covered with the hairs. They trap air in between them, a bit like the hairs on your skin. When a liquid, such as ketchup, coffee or tea, falls onto the fabric, the trapped air props it up. The liquid forms into beads and rolls safely off the fabric.

Thanks to nanowhiskers, this spilled orange juice won't soak in to leave a stain. It forms into beads and rolls off the fabric.

212

Foggy future

Scientists could fill our future with fog – a fog made up of microscopic, twelve-armed machines. They could release the machines into the air and program them to join together in a variety of ways. Depending on how they join together, the machines could form almost any common objects, such as clothes, telephones, computers, cars and even houses.

Microscopic machines like these could be programmed to link arms to form materials of any shape or form.

This computer image shows how a nanobot might be used to inject medicines into an infected body cell.

Mini-motors

The world's smallest electrical device is a motor so tiny that 100 million of them could fit onto the end of a pin. In the future, the motor might be used to power tiny robots that could travel through your bloodstream to repair damaged cells or destroy tumours.

INTERNET LINK
For a link to a website where you can watch a video-introduction to nanotechnology, go to
www.usborne-quicklinks.com

IN THE GENES

What all living things look like and how they function is largely down to their genes. These are like instruction manuals inside each human, animal and plant. Genes are sections of DNA – a chemical code that stores whole libraries of information.

DNA detectives

Your DNA is unique. This means that, unless you have an identical twin, no other living thing has exactly the same chemical code as you. The police can use this fact to help them catch criminals. They search crime scenes for evidence such as hair, blood or saliva, which can be analysed to find its DNA. If this matches DNA taken from a suspect, the police have strong evidence that the suspect was at the crime scene.

Although they look like weird, alien trees, these are hairs on a human head (the colours are added by computer). The root of each hair holds a genetic code specific to its owner.

Cracking the code

In 2000, a group of scientists announced that they had identified all the parts of the code for human life that is stored in human DNA. The code contains information about how a person is made and how he or she will grow and develop. Identifying all its parts was no easy task – it is around three billion letters long, with each letter representing one of four chemicals. Using the code, scientists hope to find out lots more about how the body works and what makes it go wrong. They have already discovered which genes contribute to asthma, diabetes and even migraines.

DNA has a long, thin shape like a twisted ladder. This computer model shows just a tiny section of DNA.

This pattern is a computer image of the code for a small sample of DNA. Each fragment of DNA is shown as a band of colour.

Pass it on

When living things reproduce, their genes are passed on to their offspring. To influence what the next generation will look like, farmers and scientists can select the types of plant or animal they want to reproduce. For example, farmers might pick only the biggest animals to breed with each other, so that their young are more likely to be big too. This is called selective breeding.

You won't find hairless rats like this one in the wild – they are the result of selective breeding. Scientists use hairless rats to test medicines and cosmetics.

Cut and paste

Technology is now so advanced that scientists can "cut" a gene out of one plant or animal and "paste" it into another, to change the way this organism looks or behaves. This is called genetic engineering, or genetic modification, and has already brought lots of advances in farming and medicine. For example, tomato plants have been modified to be poisonous to the type of beetle that would normally eat them.

GM future?

Genetic engineers are working on many life-saving projects, such as modifying pig organs so they can be given to people who need organ transplants. But some people think that there should be laws restricting what scientists can do. This is because no one knows for certain what long-term effect genetically engineered products will have on people's health or on the environment.

INTERNET LINK
For a link to a website with a video about genetically engineered green-eyed frogs, go to www.usborne-quicklinks.com

Gene

Genes are found inside cells – the tiny units that make up all living things. A gene can be taken out of a cell (shown here in yellow)...

... and placed inside a cell (shown here in blue) belonging to another living thing. The gene will affect the way the cell works in the future.

CLEVER CELLS

All living things, also called organisms, are made up of cells. Some simple organisms have just one cell, while complex organisms, like humans, have millions. Most cells contain DNA, which has all the information the cell needs to do its job. There is a whole branch of science dedicated to finding new ways to use cells in reproduction and to cure diseases.

Cloning around

Cloning is copying a living organism's DNA to create a new organism. In 1996, the first mammal clone – Dolly the sheep – was born. To make a lamb, you normally need a sperm cell from a male sheep and an egg cell from a female sheep. But scientists made Dolly in a laboratory by copying her mother's DNA. There was a problem, though. Because Dolly was born with exactly the same DNA as her six-year-old mother, her cells showed signs of early ageing. Sheep usually live for 11 or 12 years, but Dolly died at the age of six, from lung disease, which is more common in older sheep.

Udder cell

Egg cell

Egg cell emptied of DNA

The nucleus, which holds DNA, is taken from a cell in the mother's udder and put into an emptied egg cell from another sheep. The egg is put into a third sheep. The lamb is a clone of the mother.

DNA is being taken out of an animal cell through a fine needle. Only DNA that is undamaged can be used to make new animals.

Why clone?

Cloning is useful in medical research, where scientists need to try out different experiments on organisms that have exactly the same genetic make-up. In the future, cloning might even be used to bring extinct animals back to life. We might not be walking around with dinosaurs right away though, as we would need to find a dinosaur's complete, undamaged DNA.

This group of cells is the beginnings of a baby. It is just 40 hours old. The cells are ready to transform into any type of human body cell.

Job-seeking cells

When a baby has just begun to grow inside its mother, its cells are waiting to be given a job. They are called stem cells and can be programmed to become any type of body cell. As the baby grows, more and more of its stem cells are programmed. Adults have just a few stem cells left, inside their brain, bone marrow, and fat tissue.

INTERNET LINK
For a link to a website about cloning and stem cells, go to www.usborne-quicklinks.com

Cell control

Scientists are trying to control how stem cells are programmed so that they can use them to repair parts of the body, treat all kinds of illnesses, and even make replacement organs. Bone marrow stem cells are already used to treat blood diseases like leukemia. In the future, stem cells might be able to provide a cure for cancer.

Stem cells can be used to treat certain types of cancer. Scientists attach poisons to the stem cells, which can then hunt down and destroy the cancerous cells. In this image, a bone marrow stem cell (yellow) is attacking a cancer cell (orange).

BODY MECHANICS

Over the past ten years, there have been huge advances in technology and in the knowledge of how the human body works. This is helping scientists to find new ways to combine human intelligence with the power of machines.

Robot bodies

Cyborgs are humans that have machine parts built into their bodies. This may sound like science fiction, but machines such as pacemakers, which keep the heart beating regularly, and artificial limbs are currently being fitted into humans to repair their bodies. The machines are controlled by electrical signals, also called impulses, that the body uses to send messages to and from the brain. In the future, people might be able to have computers fitted into their bodies to make their senses more powerful. They could even have very tiny computers injected into their bodies to repair damaged cells.

Electronic eel

Scientists have developed a robot that is controlled by the brain of an eel. The brain is kept alive in salty water and is attached to the robot by wires. It sends electrical signals to control the direction the robot moves. This research could help in the development of robotic body parts for stroke victims and others who suffer nerve damage.

Part-man, part-machine: in the future, parts of people's bodies could perhaps be replaced by machines, like this.

1. A light turns on.

2. The robot's electronic eyes sense the light.

5. The robot goes to the light.

Computer

Eel brain

3. The robot sends a signal to the eel brain via a computer.

4. The eel brain sends a signal back to the robot.

Mind over matter

Scientists have trained a monkey to control a robot arm using just the power of its mind. When the monkey thinks about moving an object, the electrical impulses from its brain are sent to a computer, which uses the impulses to move the robot arm. In the future, this method could be used to help paralysed people move by sending their thought signals from a computerized implant in their brain to another one in their limb.

As the monkey thinks about moving an image of a ball on a screen, sensors attached to its head send electrical signals to a computer. The computer picks up the signals and uses them to make a robotic arm pick up the ball.

INTERNET LINK
For a link to a website about technology and the human body, go to www.usborne-quicklinks.com

This surfer is riding virtual ocean waves, created by a computer. His helmet is connected to the computer and controls what he sees and hears.

Virtual world

Virtual reality takes you into a world where everything you see, hear and – in the more advanced programs – feel is created by a computer. As computers become increasingly sophisticated, virtual worlds are becoming more realistic. The latest technology combines virtual reality with video cameras, so real people in different places can meet, talk to each other and even go shopping in a virtual environment.

219

INDEX

The numbers shown in **bold** type show where major subject areas are covered.

221

ACKNOWLEDGEMENTS

Cover design by Michael Hill
Additional designs by Candice Whatmore and Reuben Barrance
Additional illustrations by Ian Jackson, David Quinn, Chris Shields and Nigel Frey
Digital imagery by Keith Furnival and Joanne Kirkby
Website adviser: Lisa Watts

Every effort has been made to trace the copyright holders of the material in this book. If any rights have been omitted, the publishers offer to rectify this in any future edition, following notification. The publishers are grateful to the following organizations and individuals for their contribution and permission to reproduce this material.
t=top, b=bottom, m=middle, l=left, r=right

Cover (tl) ©Mehau Kulyk/Science Photo Library, (tr) ©D. Hurst/Alamy, (br) ©[apply pictures]/Alamy, (bl) ©Ingo Arndt/naturepl.com; Endpapers ©Mehau Kulyk/Science Photo Library; 0-1 ©Bloom Works Inc./Alamy; 2–3 ©Claude Nuridsany & Maria Perennou/Science Photo Library; 4-5 ©Pascal Goetgheluck/Science Photo Library; 6-7 ©Kenneth Libbrecht; 8-9 ©David Aubrey/CORBIS; 10 ©David Aubrey/CORBIS; 11(b) ©Naturfoto Honal/CORBIS, (tl) ©Farrell Grehan/CORBIS; 12 ©Amos Nachoum/CORBIS; 13(mr) ©Fred Winner/Jacana/Science Photo Library; 14 ©David A. Northcott/CORBIS; 15(t) ©David A. Northcott/CORBIS; 16 ©Steve Kaufman/CORBIS; 16–17(main) ©Kim Taylor/Bruce Coleman Collection; 18©Gallo Images/CORBIS; 19 ©Randy Wells/CORBIS; 20 ©Joe McDonald/Bruce Coleman Collection; 21 ©Gary Vestal/Bruce Coleman Collection; 22 ©Kevin Schafer/CORBIS; 23 ©Robert Pickett/CORBIS; 24 ©Jonathan Blair/CORBIS; 25 ©F.S. Westmorland/Science Photo Library; 26–27(main) ©Joe McDonald/CORBIS; 27(br) ©NHPA/Stephen Dalton; 28–29(main) ©Roy Morsch/CORBIS; 29(tr) ©Bob & Clara Calhoun/Bruce Coleman Collection; 30–31(b) ©Getty Images/Mitchell Funk; 31(m) ©Adam Jones/Bruce Coleman Collection; 32–33(t) ©Dr. John Brackenbury/Science Photo Library, (b) ©Martin Dohrn/Science Photo Library; 34 ©Getty Images/Angelo Cavalli; 35 ©Lester Lefkowitz/CORBIS; 36 ©DY Riess MD/Alamy; 37 ©Getty Images/Steven Hunt; 38 ©Roy Toft/National Geographic Image Collection; 39 ©Getty Images/Oliver Strewe; 40 ©Mary Ann McDonald/CORBIS; 41 ©Wolfgang Kaehler/CORBIS; 42 ©John Conrad/CORBIS; 43 ©Kevin Schafer/CORBIS; 44 ©Eye of Science/Science Photo Library; 45 ©Anthony Bannister, Gallo Images/CORBIS; 46 ©Martin Harvey, Gallo Images/CORBIS; 47 ©Dr Jeremy Burgess/Science Photo Library; 48 ©Jeffrey L. Rotman/CORBIS; 49 ©Getty Images/Mark Conlin; 50 ©Digital Vision; 51 ©Getty Images/Steve Satushek; 52–53(t) ©David A. Harvey/National Geographic Image Collection; 53(b) ©Wolfgang Kaehler/CORBIS; 54 ©John Conrad/CORBIS; 55(b) ©Digital Vision; 56 ©Darlyne A. Dr. Murawski/National Geographic Image Collection; 57(t) ©Buddy Mays/CORBIS, (b) ©Chris Mattison, Frank Lane Picture Agency/CORBIS; 58(l) ©Neil Lucas/Naturepl; 59 ©Art Wolfe/Science Photo Library; 60(b) ©Jeffrey L. Rotman/CORBIS; 61(tr) ©ImageState.com; 62 ©Norbert Rosing/National Geographic Image Collection; 63(t) ©Whitehead, Fred/Animals Animals/Earth Scenes; 64 ©Clem Haagner, Gallo Images/CORBIS; 65 ©Lynda Richardson/CORBIS; 66 ©NHPA/Haroldo Palo Jr; 67 ©Dr Karl Lounatmaa/Science Photo Library; 68 ©Ralph A. Clevenger/CORBIS; 69(t) ©Michael & Patricia Fogden/CORBIS, (b) ©George D. Lepp/CORBIS; 70 ©Getty Images/Gail Shumway; 71(t) ©Claude Nuridsany & Marie Perennou/Science Photo Library, (b) ©Wolfgang Kaehler/CORBIS; 72(tl) ©Getty Images/Steven Hunt; 72–73(b) ©Digital Vision; 73(t) ©Getty Images/Gary Bell; 74–75(b) ©Getty Images/Kevin Schafer; 75(t) ©George Grall/National Geographic Image Collection; 76 ©Willis, Gladden William/Animals Animals/Earth Scenes; 77 ©Michael S. Yamashita/CORBIS; 78 ©David Kjaer/Naturepl; 79 ©Anup Shah/Naturepl; 80(b) ©Australian Picture Library/Leo Meier; 80–81(t) ©Digital Vision; 82(t) ©Jonathan Smith, Cordaiy Photo Library Ltd/CORBIS, (b) ©Digital Vision; 83 ©Kevin Schafer/CORBIS; 84 ©Getty Images/Peter David; 85(t) ©Anthony Bannister, Gallo Images/CORBIS; 86 ©David A. Northcott/CORBIS; 87(t), (ml) ©David A. Northcott/CORBIS, (mr) ©Martin Harvey, Gallo Images/CORBIS; 88(tr) ©Robert Pickett/CORBIS, (b) ©Tim Davis/CORBIS; 89 ©Roy Morsch/CORBIS; 90 ©Getty Images/ Manoj Shah; 91 ©Martin Harvey, Gallo Images/CORBIS; 92 ©Gray Hardel/CORBIS; 93 ©NHPA/G. Bernard; 94 ©John Holmes, Frank Lane Picture Agency/CORBIS; 95 ©Gary W. Carter/CORBIS; 96 ©Royalty-Free/CORBIS; 97 ©Jeffrey L. Rotman/CORBIS; 98 ©Chris Mattison, Frank Lane Picture Agency/CORBIS; 99 ©Stephen Frink/CORBIS; 100 ©Joe McDonald/CORBIS; 101(t) Getty Images/Laurence Hughes, (b) ©Kennan Ward/CORBIS; 102 ©Torleif Svensson/CORBIS; 103 ©Martin Harvey, Gallo Images/CORBIS; 104–105(main) ©Anthony Bannister, Gallo Images/CORBIS; 105(br) ©Anthony Bannister, Gallo Images/CORBIS; 106 ©William Manning/CORBIS; 107 ©Royalty-Free/CORBIS; 108 ©Paulo De Oliveira/OSF; 109 ©Paul A. Zahl/National Geographic Image Collection; 110 ©Chris Mattison, Frank Lane Picture Agency/CORBIS; 111 ©Martin Harvey, Gallo Images/CORBIS; 112(t) ©Digital Vision; 112–113(b) ©Getty Images/Wolfgang Kaehler; 114(b) ©Tom Brakefield/CORBIS; 115(t) ©Tom Brakefield/CORBIS, (br) Michael S. Quinton/National Geographic Image Collection; 116 ©Michael Fogden/OSF; 117 (m) ©Michael & Patricia Fogden/CORBIS, (br) Richard T. Nowitz/CORBIS; 118 ©Getty Images/Christoph Burki; 119(t) ©Andrew Syred/Science Photo Library, (b) ©Patrick Johns/CORBIS; 120 ©Peter Scoones/Science Photo Library; 121 ©Jeffrey L. Rotman/CORBIS; 122–123 ©Frank Lane Picture Agency/CORBIS; 123 ©David A. Northcott/CORBIS; 124(t) ©Levin, Ted/Animals Animals/Earth Scenes, (b) ©Digital Vision; 125 ©Andrew Syred/Science Photo Library; 126(t) ©Digital Vision, (b) ©Habicht, Michael/Animals Animals/Earth Scenes; 127 ©Dick, Michael/Animals Animals/Earth Scenes; 128 ©John Mitchell/Science Photo Library; 129(t) ©NHMPL/Science Photo Library, (b) ©OSF/Animals Animals/Earth Scenes; 130-131 ©Lawrence Lawry/Science Photo Library; 132(b) ©O. Louis Mazzatenta/National Geographic Image Collection; 133(t) ©Alexis Rosenfeld/Science Photo Library; 135 Courtesy of the IBM Almaden Research Center; 136 ©Arnold Fisher/Science Photo Library; 137 ©Charles D. Winters/Science Photo Library; 138 (main) ©Mehau Kulyk/Science Photo Library, (ml) ©Fermilab/Science Photo Library; 139(t) ©Thomas Tegge/Lawrence Livermore National Laboratory; 140(b) Garth Williams, Mark Pfeifer & Ian Robinson, Advanced Photon Source national research facility, University of Illinois, Chicago, USA; 141(t) ©Geoff Tompkinson/Science Photo Library; 142(t) Image courtesy of Michael Pique, The Scripps Research Institute, (bl) ©Geoff Tompkinson/Science Photo Library; 143(b) ©Roger Harris/Science Photo Library; 144 ©The Abstract Archive; 145(br) ©Dynamic Graphics/John Foxx Images Collection; 146(m) ©Dr. Jeremy Burgess/Science Photo Library; (b) ©Lee D. Simon/Science Photo Library; 147(t) ©James Bell/Science Photo Library, 147(br) ©NASA/Marshall Space Flight Center; 148(l) ©Richard Megna/Fundamental Photos/Science Photo Library; 149(t) Dr. Jeremy Burgess/Science Photo Library, (b) ©Philips; 150(main) ©Lawrence Berkeley Laboratory/Science Photo Library, (br) Image provided by the Department of Molecular & Medical Pharmacology, David Geffen School of Medicine at UCLA. Copyright © 1994-2004 Let's Play PET, Crump Institute for Molecular Imaging; 151(tl) ©Digital Vision, (br) ©Lawrence Berkeley National Laboratory; 152 ©Kenneth Libbrecht; 152–153(background) ©Digital Vision; 153 ©Powerstock; 154(tl) ©ImageState/Alamy, (m) ©2004 Lord Corporation. All rights reserved, (br) ©Pascal Goetgheluck/Science Photo Library; 155(t) Courtesy of the National Physical Laboratory, (r) ©SCPhotos/Alamy; 156(l) ©Eye of Science/Science Photo Library; 157(t) ©Dr. Chris Somerville/Science Photo Library; 158(t) ©Alfred Pasieka/Science Photo Library, (b) ©Forhistorisk Museum, Denmark/Munoz-Yague/Science Photo Library; 159(tr) ©David Luzzi, University of Pennsylvania/Science Photo Library; 160 ©Getty Images/NHMPL; 161 Courtesy NASA/JPL-Caltech; 162(main) ©Lawrence Lawry/Science Photo Library; 163(tm) ©NaturePicks/Alamy, (tr) © Andrew Syred/Science Photo Library, (b) ©PHOTOTAKE Inc./Alamy; 164 ©PHOTOTAKE Inc./Alamy; 165(b) ©Yann Arthus-Bertrand/CORBIS; 166–167 ©Getty Images/Tom Mareschal; 167(br) ©CORBIS SYGMA; 168 ©Digital Vision; 169(br) ©Mehau Kulyk/Science Photo Library; 170–171 ©Joe McBride/CORBIS; 171(tr) ©Mehau Kulyk/Science Photo Library; 172(tr) ©Bettmann/CORBIS, (bl) ©Digital Vision; 173 ©Roger Harris/Science Photo Library; 174 ©Science Photo Library; 175(tr) ©NASA, (bl) ©Matthew Oldfield, Scubazoo/Science Photo Library; 176(b) ©David Fleetham/OSF; 177 ©US Department of Defense/Science Photo Library: photograph by John Gay; 178(main) ©NHPA/Stephen Dalton, (br) ©GE Healthcare; 179 ©W. Haxby, Lamont-Doherty Earth Observatory/Science Photo Library; 180 ©Brand X Pictures/Alamy; 181(r) ©NASA/JPL-Caltech, (bl) ©Keith Kent/Science Photo Library; 182(t) ©Alexander Tsiaras/Science Photo Library; 183(b) ©Gabe Palmer/CORBIS; 184(b) ©David Taylor/Science Photo Library; 185(t) ©Manfred Kage/Science Photo Library; 186(main) ©Adam Hart-Davis/Science Photo Library, (br) ©Charles D. Winters/Science Photo Library; 187(tl) ©Peter Menzel/Science Photo Library, (br) ©Peter Menzel/Science Photo Library; 188 ©MPI Biochemistry/Volker Steger/Science Photo Library; 189(t) ©Zephyr/Science Photo Library; 190(t) ©James King-Holmes/Science Photo Library, (br) ©Cordelia Molloy/Science Photo Library; 191 ©Simon Fraser/Royal Victoria Infirmary, Newcastle upon Tyne/Science Photo Library; 191 ©NASA; 192 ©Richard Cummins/CORBIS; 194(bl) ©Max-Planck-Institut für Radioastronomie/Science Photo Library; 195(main) ©British Technical Films/Science Photo Library, (ml) Private Art Collection; 196 ©Roger Ressmeyer/CORBIS; 197(tr) ©Dynamic Graphics/John Foxx Images Collection, (r) ©Ted Mahieu/CORBIS; 198 ©Tek Image/Science Photo Library; 199(t) ©Photo by Long Island Laser Works, Inc. www.lilaser.net; 200 ©Theo Allofs/CORBIS; 201(tr) ©VVG/Science Photo Library, (bl) ©Dr Jeremy Burgess/Science Photo Library, (b) ©Bjørn Rørslett-NN/Nærfoto; 202(m) Based on figure by Edgar Rubin, (mr) Based on a figure by Edwin G. Boring, (bl) Image created using 3D Miracle software by Media Programming; 203(t) ©Akiyoshi Kitaoka 2003, (bl) Image by R. C. James, (bm) Used by permission of Edward H. Adelson, (br) ©Akiyoshi Kitaoka 1998; 204(main) ©Siemens Press Photo; 205(tr) ©Reuters/CORBIS, (br) ©Getty Images/Willie Maldonado; 206–207(Background) ©Digital Vision; 207 ©Herrmann/Starke/CORBIS; 208(br) ©Mauro Fermariello/Science Photo Library; 209(tr) ©David Parker/Science Photo Library; 210(Main) ©Peter Menzel/Science Photo Library, (br) Illustration based on photography, MIT CSAIL; 211 (ml) Image produced courtesy of Tmsuk Co. Ltd and Waseda University, Japan, (br) ©Randy Montoya, Sandia National Laboratories; 212 ©Dr Tony Brain/Science Photo Library; 213 ©Roger Harris/Science Photo Library; 214(main) ©VVG/Science Photo Library; 215(main) ©Getty Images/G. Robert Bishop; 216(r) ©M. Baret, Rapho/Science Photo Library; 217(tr) ©Dr G. Moscoso/Science Photo Library, (br) ©Eye of Science/Science Photo Library; 218(l) ©Peter Menzel/Science Photo Library; 219(main) ©Image Source/Alamy.